EXILE IS MY HOME

FOUR PLAYS BY DOMNICA RADULESCU

NoPassport Press

Exile is my home: Four Plays by Domnica Radulescu

Volume copyright 2020.

Foreword by Julia Pascal,

copyright Julia Pascal 2020.

Introduction by Christine Evans,

copyright Christine Evans 2020.

For performance rights enquiries for all plays in this volume contact the author at domnicaradulescu.com

NoPassport Press (founding editor: Caridad Svich)

PO Box 1786, South Gate, CA 90280 USA.

Website: https://www.nopassport.org

Email: NoPassportPress@aol.com

ISBN: 978-1-71685-732-4

To the Memory of Cecilia (Mimi) Radulescu

Whose love of theater seeped into my own blood

TABLE OF CONTENTS

ACKNOWLEDGMENTS

The plays gathered in this volume have been conceived, created and developed over a decade in the interstices between my practical work in the theater as director and educator on one hand and my work as a creative fiction writer and scholar on the other hand. They have emerged from clashing, sometimes wrenching or haunting realities, experiences, and searches. Many entities and individuals have contributed to bringing them to the shape they are in the present volume.

I owe a large debt of gratitude to Washington and Lee University for the Lenfest summer grants that I have received over the past several years and for the sabbatical leaves of absence which have afforded me the time and travel opportunities that have fueled some of these theatrical works.

I offer profuse thanks to the theater directors and educators who have directed staged readings or productions of these plays and have brought them to life in creative and innovative ways. I thank Marcy Arlin for the developmental readings of *Exile Is My Home* at TheaterLab in New York city. I thank Andreas Robertz for his brilliant direction of *Exile Is My Home* at Theater for the New City in New York and to the entire cast of actors who rightfully deserved the Outstanding Performance by an Ensemble Cast Award from the Hispanic Organization of Latin Actors.

I thank Rachel Lewis for teaching my plays *Exile Is My Home* and *The Town with Very Nice People* in several of her theater and gender studies courses at George Mason University, and Catalina Iliescu Gheorghiu for teaching *Exile is My Home* at the

University of Alicante, Spain and organizing several staged readings as well as for her beautiful translation into Spanish of the same play. I equally thank Carol Campbell for the inspired direction of several staged readings of *Exile Is My Home* and *The Town with Very Nice People* at George Mason University and at other venues in Virginia. I also thank Catalina Florescu for teaching and writing about *Exile Is My Home*. I owe a debt of gratitude to Emma Goldman-Sherman and her WriteNow writing workshop which has contributed to the development and polishing of the plays *Crossings* and *House in a Boat*.

I also wish to thank the actors who have consistently lent their passion and talents to the interpretations of the roles in productions and readings of these plays over the years, and in particular Nikaury Rodriguez, Mario Golden and Florinda Ruiz.

I am grateful to my partner Henry who has offered unfaltering support and precious help to all the productions and readings of my plays. I thank my son Alexander Tanson for the powerful and haunting music he composed for the production of *Exile Is My Home* and which has practically become inseparable from the full appreciation and substance of the play.

I offer warm thanks and gratitude to Veronica, "la reina de los immigrantes de Lexington," for the precious help with the interviews and with gathering the refugees' stories.

I am extremely grateful to Caridad Svich for having undertaken the publication of this volume, for her impeccable editorial work, and particularly for forging ahead, undeterred by the difficulties associated with a global pandemic.

FOREWORD

Domnica Radulescu came on to my radar through the International Centre for Women Playwrights. We connected through our Romanian heritage. When I read her work, I was astounded by her wild, witty and daring style, so when she approached me to write this Foreword, I immediately agreed.

There is a word in Yiddish which cannot be translated into English. *Meschuggah.* It encapsulates a sense of craziness, anarchy and an unbound imagination. This word comes to mind when reading Radulescu but her work is not merely meschuggah, her dramas are filled with iconoclastic impulses that are political, philosophical and ecological.

Radulescu's writing sits within the larger canon of European exiles. Her sister writers are Eva Hoffman, Marianne Hirsch, Nadine Fresco – all carry the Old Country on their backs and wrestle with the history of statelessness, abandon and loss. But Hoffman, Hirsch and Fresco are not playwrights and so how can Radulescu's work be framed? Or can it be? It would be easy to see Radulescu as the literary great granddaughter of her fellow Romanian playwright Eugène Ionescu and particularly in regard to his play *Rhinoceros*. But Radulescu's feminist vision adds another level of politics as well as that of her anti-fascism. Her plays are profoundly philosophical anti-authoritarian feminist narratives that out-Ionesco Ionesco in their theatricality.

In Exile Is My Home. A Sci-fi Immigrant Fairy Tale Radulescu creates a satire on nationalism and man-made borders. The philosophy behind the work is complex and is supported by psychological studies. I was struck by the particular vision

Radulescu brings to the concept of emigration. The image of humans carrying their homes on their backs, like snails, is a perfect symbol of rootlessness and exile. I loved this play's interrogation of memory and its refusal to be nostalgic about The Old Country. A woman speaks of her grandparents. 'They made me yearn for something, but I don't know what'. But longing for the past is never utopic. As Mina, the eternal immigrant, says 'That's the problem with memory and storytelling: it makes you yearn for the past even if that past was shitty and it makes you want a home'.

The Town with Very Nice People. A Strident Immigrant Operetta, Radulescu dares to critique feminism as a religion which shames other feminists who do not follow the party line. Again, there is this sense of a hugely individual voice and great intelligence that refuses the binary, the simplistic and the politically correct.

Throughout the works in this volume there are questions that the theatre director in me asks. Radulescu's sense of absurdism has me laughing out loud but how would I stage it?

In House in a Boat with Food and No God. A Nomadic Dystopia on Water she creates a scenography that is on and under water. It is cartoon-like in its playful toying with the grotesque. A parthenogenetic child is a tomato or a potato and therefore food is always present. A woman has a hundred vaginas because God, 'a racist, atheist and a vampire pig' has killed so many children and she must make up the loss. My question about scenography was answered when I realized that either I would need a brilliant designer, or I would have the stage directions read out as a way of evoking Radulescu's extraordinary imagination.

A sense of loss is the pervading theme that unites all the texts. *Crossings: A Play of Immigrant Voices* is a more austere text using a choral, bilingual form to reveal the horror of Donald Trump's cruel anti-immigration laws. This is a scream of protest against the way immigrants from across the border are treated and its power is huge. The range of Radulescu's creativity is easy to appreciate in this fascinating volume of plays. I doubt if they will date as long as patriarchy and xenophobia exist.

Julia Pascal, award winning playwright and director, NESTA Dreamtime Fellow, author of *The Holocaust Trilogy, Woman in the Moon* and many other plays.

INTRODUCTION

by Christine Evans

In *Exile Is My Home,* the titular play of this collection, the interplanetary traveling companions Mina and Lina discuss their origins:

LINA: I was born in exile. Where were you born?

MINA: I was born on the way to the market.

They agree that they get along better than those who "were born somewhere precise," who are always "such sticklers for geography." And indeed, sticklers for geography will find their version of the world--its borders and orders--rudely shaken, challenged, laughed at and radically rewritten in these plays. Middle-aged Lina and Mina frolic on their interplanetary travels with the two remaining survivors of the War of the Penises: the Man with Large Penis and the Man with Small Penis. Faced with patriarchal wreckage, they repopulate the planet: playful intention spews forth new "brown babies," new, fecund realities.

Domnica Radulescu's antic pageantry dismisses bourgeois realism as the possession of those with homes, born "somewhere precise." For her characters, life is instead chaotic, unpredictable, tragi-comic, haunted and raddled by the competing pulls of memory and forgetting. Her characters exhume, revive, re-populate the borderlands, refusing either to occupy a pious victimhood or give up on the complex, impossible pursuit of home. They traverse the uninhabitable sphere of what Giorgio Agamben calls the "zone of exception," that contradictory space ruled by and yet outside of the law, carved out by the State to preserve its sovereignty. Most subversively, they are women, immigrants, refugees, middle-aged: figures who occupy their own zone of exception in relation to white-supremacist patriarchal use value.

Radulescu's plays are carnivalesque, grotesquely comic, savagely sad and breath-taking in their imaginative scope. They bound over oceans, continents, planets, stifling small-town faculty meetings and the terrifying liminal spaces of the US border. From the "sci-fi immigrant fairy tale" of *Exile Is My Home,* to the scathingly satirical comedy-of-manners of *The Town with Very Nice People,* to the anti-creation myth of *House in a Boat with Food and No God,* Radulescu's heroines are "Femi-freed," multi-colored, loud-mouthed and hybrid. They subvert received pieties, purities and borders, which they astutely peg as the linchpins of fascist and genocidal regimes.

While post-dramatic, Radulescu's work also harks back to older forms that move through both figurative and literal landscapes: pageants, processions, Passion Plays. As in the Medieval morality play *Everyman,* the dangerous terrain her characters traverse is spiked with moral dangers, sloughs of despond, shape-shifting assailants. The Woman Who Eats Hearts morphs into Planet America's Very White Hitler-Loving Woman, and they both spew forth anti-immigrant, genocidal, racial-purity fantasies:

> WOMAN WHO EATS HEARTS [...] I once was a woman and ate her, vomit on you and your filthy multiculturalism. I once was head of state, mother fucking head of state in Indochina, then the war came, then another war came, then I started ethnic

cleansing, too many races instead of just one, too many colors instead of just one, ethnic cleansing felt good, such a relief, all was going well on the planet and I had many juicy hearts waiting to be eaten, fuck, shit, cunt, ethnic cleansing, long live genocide, die, die, die.

The first three plays in the collection gleefully stage such stream-of-consciousness outpourings, giving imaginative voice to the obscene political fantasies that police all kinds of borders. However, the final play in this collection, *Crossings: A Play of Immigrant Voices* showcases a different register of Radulescu's voice. Her outsider's eye, empathy and rage at injustice are channeled into an artful polyphony, drawn from interviews with immigrants from Mexico, Guatemala and Honduras who now live and work in Virginia. Radulescu orchestrates their border narratives of terror, love, loss and reinvention into a bilingual choreo-poem that retains the specificity of each voice, while creating resonance between them through the interwoven elements of narration and chorus.

Domnica Radulescu is a writer of radical imagination and heart with the signature clownish melancholy of the Eastern European exile, who knows in her bones that countries, memories, and the lived sense of home, precariously anchored through the everyday, can burn away in any moment. While often very funny, hers are savage plays that refuse the peculiarly American obsession with uplifting endings.

All the more reason, then, to treasure this unique collection, which allows the reader to stage Radulescu's wild, comical, obscene and tragic plays in that secret landscape, the theatre of the mind.

Christine Evans is an award-winning playwright, author of *You Are Dead You Are Here*, *Trojan Barbie* and many other plays, is the recipient of numerous fellowships and prizes among which the Jane Chambers Playwriting Award (2007), The Bogliasco Foundation Fellowship, the RISCA Merit Award.

Exile Is My Home. A Sci-fi Immigrant Fairy-Tale

Runner up in the 2014 Jane Chambers Playwriting Competition

Jane Chambers Playwriting Award Jury noted: "moving, epic, feminist, and comedic, this highly theatrical play evokes the human, social and political complexities of exile with depth, humor and adaptive re-invention."

Nominated for the New York Innovative Theater Awards-April/May 2016

Development History

This play was developed first as a staged reading under the direction of Marcy Arlin of the Immigrant Theater Project, at TheaterLab off, off Broadway in October 2014.

It was produced at Theater for the New City in New York City, directed by Andreas Robertz in April and May of 2016. The production of *Exile Is My Home* at Theater for the New City won the HOLA Award for Outstanding Performance by an Ensemble Cast.

Industry Reviews:

"From the get-go, the new play "Exile is my Home" written by Domnica Radulescu, and directed by Andreas Robertz, captivated the intimate crowd at the Theater for the New City. This play tells the story of Mina (Noemi de la Puente) and Lina (Nikaury Rodriguez). They are a refugee couple from the Balkans that travel through the cosmos in search of a place called home. The music and lights captured the initial attention of the audience member initially, but it is the important and socially conscious storyline that leaves a lasting imprint.

Although Mina and Lina traveled to different galaxies and far-away places, the all-too familiar themes of war, subsequent displacement, and uprooting of people serve as a painful reminder of the reality we currently face here on earth. With just seven cast members, and modest stage props, the story was still told and without limitation. As a member of the audience, I was taken to another place. A different world, a far-away galaxy, yet still strangely familiar to the one I know.

Notable performances were given by Mirandy Rodgriguez, who provided necessary comic relief as a Guatemalan Massage Therapist. Vivienne Jurado provided a remarkable performance playing various characters ranging from naïve to charming, to complete evil. Director Andreas Robertz knows himself what it is like to miss one's homeland, having come from Germany. He does a great job embracing a diversity of voices in this production, with an openness to taking a risk and trying something completely different. All throughout, the music of Alexander Tanson provided an appropriate mix of sonic dissonance, and out-of-the-world sounds. Of the many topics addressed, both subtle and direct, despite the vast contrast of their environment, Mina and Lina faced the same universal social issues. Gender, sexuality, feminism, drug addiction, human rights, it's all there in this story. Playful and creative, but also painfully true to the realities faced by millions every day. A place called home is what we are searching for, not just for the play's main characters, but for all of us as well. "Exile is my Home" emanates a powerful story with a creative edge.
Frederick R. Stal, for *RG Magazine*, May 4th, 2016.

"*Exile Is My Home,* a provocative new play by internationally renowned author Domnica Radulescu. Told as a sci-fi, post-apocalyptic fairy tale, *Exile Is My Home* is the haunting story of Mina and Lina, a refugee couple from the Balkans traveling through the galaxy in search of a planet to call home. The play combines absurdist comedy, irony and suspense to raise consciousness about the current international refugee crisis and the complexity of issues related to it. The story emerged partly from Radulescu's own experience as a political refugee from the former communist dictatorship of Nicolae Ceausescu and other accounts of displacement. As millions of people are uprooted from their homes and swept across tumultuous seas and often unwelcome lands, *Exile Is My Home* highlights the importance of immigrant theater in bringing awareness about many of the challenges facing our world today." **New York Theater Review,** **May 7th, 2016.**

SETTINGS

Intergalactic Space, three different planets and Planet America.

TIME

A Dystopian Present. Flashbacks to the past.

CHARACTERS

MINA: A woman in her fifties, of unclear profession, artistic, bohemian, flamboyant and temperamental. She is an émigré from the country of Lugubria where they speak French and Finish and maybe Latvian or Lithuanian.

LINA: A woman in her sixties, and of the very clear profession of urban planning, elegant, precise, yet sentimental. She is an émigré from a Balkan country where they speak Romanian, Polish and Hungarian and maybe Slovenian or Slovakian.

GIRL ON THE FIRST PLANET: A young woman in her twenties who is a massage therapist and works on tired bodies who have landed on her planet from Planet America, or from a West European country or an East European country. She is one of the last survivors on her planet. She is not an émigré but was born on the first planet. In the last act she becomes GUATEMALAN MASSAGE THERAPIST.

MAN WITH SMALL PENIS: One of only two survivors of the war of the penises on The First Planet. In the last act he becomes TAXI DRIVER FROM UZBEKISTAN.

MAN WITH LARGE PENIS: The other one of the only two survivors of the war of the penises. In the last act he becomes IRRITATED IMMIGRATION OFFICER.

GIRL ON THE SECOND PLANET: An actress who goes through her repertoire of plays in a continuous swirl of parts. She is a re-expatriated immigrant from the Planet America to the country of the Second Planet.

WOMAN WHO EATS HEARTS: An old woman who eats the hearts of lonely travelers who fall asleep or show the emotion of yearning for a home on her planet. Her planet is deceptively white and attracts lonely tired travelers. The woman is like a female version of the Minotaur, she is in constant need of human blood, particularly young hearts. In the last act she becomes VERY WHITE HITLER LOVING WOMAN.

BILLY: Son of MINA and LINA.

BULGARIAN ORGAN THIEVES I and II: Just as their name proclaims, they are part of the BULGARIAN mafia involved in human and organ trafficking.

VERY WHITE HITLER LOVING WOMAN: Hateful Informer who was reincarnated from WOMAN WHO EATS HEARTS in ACT III and persecutes all new immigrants to Planet America. She also works for TSA, NSA and ICE.

GUATEMALAN MASSAGE THERAPIST: Immigrant from The First Planet, trying to obtain legal immigration status on Planet America in ACT IV.

TAXI DRIVER FROM UZBEKISTAN: Survivor from The First Planet trying to immigrate to Planet America in ACT IV.

IRRITATED IMMIGRATION OFFICER: Angry and unpleasant immigrant hating officer in the Immigration Office on Planet America.

The play follows the journey of Mina and Lina through different planets and countries in search of a home. Throughout their journey they each carry a miniature folding house that unfolds whenever they want to settle somewhere for the night. They carry these houses on their backs like backpacks and whenever they want to settle somewhere for the night, they open them up. The houses are equipped with everything they need to be modestly comfortable. Whenever needed for their intergalactic traveling needs, these houses also function as spaceships.

Pre-show music. Eerie, stellar.

ACT I

The First Planet – Living by One's Principles

LINA: I was born in exile. Where were you born?

MINA: I was born on the way to the market.

LINA: Oh, that makes sense then, that's why we get along. Why we sort of get along. In any case, it's better than with the others who were born somewhere precise.

MINA: I know, people who were born somewhere precise are always such sticklers for geography. They say things like I was born in a little town in the country of Vdansk or the country of Smolensk, in the big city in Chesterbester, in a small house, in a big house, in a house with a big yard with a cherry orchard ...

LINA: I know what you mean, blah, blah, right? I was born here, I was born over there, I am the son/daughter/sister/brother of so and so in the Textile Industry, of so and so at the Factory of Paintbrushes. Good for us that we were born in the air.

MINA: Nowhere.

LINA: In the air.

MINA: If it wasn't so damn inconvenient to spend one's life on the road, I would say living in constant exile is the best home there is.

LINA: Were we ever stable?

MINA: I don't know, what do you remember?

LINA: I don't know, what do you remember?

MINA: I don't know, what do you remember?

LINA: I don't know, what do you fucking remember?

MINA: You don't have to get bitchy. It's hard enough we must carry these stupid houses on our backs like we were a bunch of fucking snails.

LINA: I remember a pond. A blue pond with a red flower in the middle. I was very little, and I had a mother and a father. They were not house carrying people like we are, and they had a regular house with a foundation in the ground and all. And a small potato garden in the front. My mother had always said I was born by the side of the road. After she gave birth to me she put me in her bag and carried me around for a while until she met my father and he built her a house with a foundation and a potato garden and a blue pond with a red flower in the middle.

MINA: That's a nice story Lina, I never knew that about you and your family. My mother dropped me on the way to the market in another country, as she was going to buy fruit. She crawled in the desert with me in her fruit bag right after she had given birth. She wanted to say I was born in the country of Lugubria, so when she came into the town and went to the authorities to say she was asking for asylum from bad people in her country and produced me out of her bag of fruit from the market together with guava and oranges, and said "I just gave birth to this," everybody was stunned and said I was a country citizen right away. My mother was so happy that she died on the spot.

LINA: That's an even better story than mine, Mina. I became an urban planner because the house I was brought up in right after my birth by the side of the road, was in the middle of the fucking nowhere and my mother wanted a city. She was a daughter of city people from Slovakia. I built a little city like the city of Dansk in

Slovakia for my mother. And then I left because the war started. They always start wars in that part of the world...

MINA: Hey Lina, I'm getting sort of tired from all this walking and walking across the desert. Where are we going to live today? What do you say we visit this little planet here on our right? I think it's on our list of planets to visit. Maybe they'll give us a place to sleep for the night and then if we like it enough maybe we'll stay for a while.

> *Mina and Lina travel to PLANET NUMBER ONE. They land on the planet, park their spaceship/houses on what looks like a deserted street in a devastated area filled with rubble, smashed houses, and mounds of garbage. Down the deserted street they see a small round yellow house that seems to have escaped the general devastation and is shiny and new. Intergalactic music continues until they reach the house and enter it.*

GIRL ON THE FIRST PLANET (*She greets them while dancing. She is dressed in colored rags. On one side of the house are two fancy massage tables next to one another*): It's so damned hard to live by one's principles. No wonder that people on earth kill and pillage and masturbate all over the universe.

MINA (*In a high-pitched loud voice*): Hello Girl on the First Planet. We have travelled a long way to come visit you. We crossed the deserts of Israel on camels and Nubian Goats and flew on our special mourning doves across the intergalactic highway all the way from the Planet Earth. We came here because we heard you are the expert on living by one's principles and we wanted to know how you do it.

LINA: We also want to be able to live by our principles. But mostly we want to find a home. We are tired of carrying these two houses. We want to immigrate to your planet. We speak many languages and we learn fast. We were born in exile and we adapt easily.

GIRL ON THE FIRST PLANET (*Stops her dancing in a dramatic jump landing right in front of the two women*): You've come to the right place, though don't expect to find everything exactly the way you have heard of it in the news. I was just saying: you have these beautiful colorful and perfectly built principles out there, like the principle of tolerance or the principle of respect for your fucking fellow men or women and you are hanging onto these beautiful principles as if you were hanging on to a monkey bar. Then your hands get tired, your head starts spinning and before you know it you are on the ground in pile of shit with all the other assholes. But whatever, let's think positively, the immigration process here is quite easy. The first thing you do is you let me give you a massage. That will relax your tired bodies and then you can better hang on to the monkey bar of super noble principles. And then you can settle and make a stable home here next to all the other immigrants. So first get up on this massage table here.

> *Sounds of pounding and animated massage accompany the massage music.*

GIRL ON FIRST PLANET: So, what can you two do? Can you build, rebuild, construct, destroy, rebuild again, grow things, and make things? Our planet is a little depleted right now from a recent war we've just had. The men on our planet decided to kill each other on account on the sizes of their penises. If we could at least have had a war that started out of religious intolerance, that would have been more noble; or fighting for pieces of land and territory on our already tiny planet, that would have made some sense; or even to have had a war over gold or corn or the price of gas, something crass and concrete like that, then I would have felt a little bit better about the war. But over the size of penises? I know it's so unimaginative, right? So in any case, our planet is in disarray, the houses are crumbled to the ground, our schools are in shambles, our streets are cracked and filled with potholes from the explosions and the bodies of the population are in terrible shape, disjointed, out of whack, hunched over, crippled or twisted. I restore bodies with my massage therapy. And because of my high success rate with the bodies, our planet has gotten the reputation of living by its principles. Because I deliver what I say I deliver. People leave my massage table feeling renewed. But then the next day they start arguing again and they start wars over the size of penises. Right now, our population of men has been reduced to two.

MINA AND LINA: TWO? Two men, that's all you have on your planet?

GIRL ON FIRST PLANET: Yes, TWO. Ironically, the one with the smallest penis and the one with the largest penis are the only ones who survived the previous war. Survival of the fittest, what do you want! They are both in great shape because I've massaged them until my arms were about to fall off. We have to take good care of them and protect them from all dangers and stress. They are our only chance at repopulating our planet, but the women have all written off sex for the next one hundred years. We need new flesh and blood, new seeds for a new world, and now with you two who have come to visit us all the way from Planet Exile, I think we can also rebuild our cities.

LINA: Ouch, that hurts, do you have to be so rough? In any case you've got the right people – I'm an urban planner and my friend Mina here is a bohemian artist. I can restore the cities and she can restore the arts. That is if I ever escape from this massage therapy without any torn muscles and twisted joints.

GIRL ON THE FIRST PLANET: Don't worry, nothing will break, you'll be as good as new, trust me, I deliver what I promise and live by my principles, remember?

MINA (*Acting very curious and sly*): So, where do you keep these two men? Can we maybe see them? Maybe meet them one day?

LINA *(Acting surprised by Mina's curiosity)*: Seriously? You don't mean to say you'd like a taste, a piece of these men, do you? Remember, we are on a mission, and our mission is to find the perfect home, a home for us two homeless women. And besides, you don't do those kinds of things with men. I thought you only loved me.

MINA: This has nothing to do with love. It's all about saving this planet from total extinction and trying something new we've never tried before. And I never thought you felt that way about our adorable little mobile portable homes. I thought we always had a home and we didn't want a home, home in the traditional sense but more like a planet home, a universe home, something open and indefinite where we wouldn't get stuck in all sorts of sentimental memories of the hallway to the bathroom or the window giving out to a lumber yard or shit like that which people recount from their childhoods and never get over.

GIRL ON THE FIRST PLANET (*Puts more pressure on Mina and Lina in the massage and climbs on top of them to crack their backs back into shape, a knee on each one of their backs. Cracking sounds can be heard*): I'd be glad to introduce you to them only that they are very shy, and they hide all the time. But they are up for grabs, really if you can find them. Maybe you two could rebuild and reinvigorate our town and our population with your foreign and earthly skills.

> *The massage is finished, and Mina and Lina jump off the table all light and nimble and put their clothes back on*

quickly. Girl on the First Planet walks them over to a tiny train station amidst rubble and ruins from a war. There is a deserted train car. Two men are hiding in it: one with a small penis, the other with a large penis.

LINA: Seriously, I think this is stupid, searching for these pathetic men and hoping to regenerate their planet. This is not a good home for us, it's too cliché, and too much like the crap we already have on earth.

MINA: I think it can be fun, and we can help these people with our skills of lust and performance and urban planning. They must get these two bozos out of their hiding places and try to copulate again and bring back the species, or they will all be extinct.

LINA: Because of their own stupidity, right? Whose fault is it they had the idiotic war and killed each other to almost total extinction over the sizes of their penises? Maybe they deserve to be extinct.

[margin handwritten: root of Earth's wars]

MINA: Right, because on our very smart planet Earth, nobody has ever killed each other or massacred masses of people, or waged genocidal wars for the stupidest reasons.

GIRL ON THE FIRST PLANET: All right you two, stop arguing with each other, there is enough strife everywhere already. Try to live up to your principles of good will and understanding and ride on the wave of your new massage therapy, what the fuck! And please sing that sweet Balkan song again. I thought I heard a little bit of movement in that abandoned red train car over there.

MINA: How did you know it was a Balkan song?

GIRL ON THE FIRST PLANET: My grandmother was from a Balkan country somewhere in the Carpathians. I am the first generation born on this planet. And she used to always sing sentimental Balkan songs to put me to sleep. They made me yearn for something, but I didn't know what.

[handwritten: a sense of home you're never known]

MINA: See, that's the problem with memory and storytelling: it makes you yearn for the past even if the past was shitty and it makes you want a home. I think homeless is better. I think exile is better. Those sentimental Balkan songs – the soldiers sang them in all kinds of sinister wars as they were massacring entire populations and raping women in rape hotels and getting drunk and slobbering all over their drinks to the sound of sentimental songs - Yuk! The fucking Balkans are everywhere, even out here on a different planet, you can't get rid of the fucking Balkans.

GIRL ON THE FIRST PLANET: Oh Mina, I think you need another massage, a triple dose massage, you are too bitter and disjointed. Now do you two courageous women want to save these poor men and regenerate our species or what?

LINA: Look! I think I saw a shadow moving over there in that deserted train car. Let's get on it. I've always loved trains. They remind me of something. A journey I once took. A city I once travelled to. Maybe this could be fun after all.

> *Lina and Mina get on the deserted train car. Lina sings a French song, an Edith Piaf song, sad and heart wrenching. Men's voices are heard. The two men are singing a Hungarian song. We can only see shadows through the train windows and hear animated voices, songs, and laughter. The singing, laughing, and talking sound like a drinking party.*

VOICE OF MAN WITH SMALL PENIS: Oh, so you are Hungarian too?

MINA's Voice: I am a little Hungarian, yes, I am, and Polish. I'm also Polish.

VOICE OF MAN WITH LARGE PENIS: Oh, and you are French?

LINA's Voice: I am a little bit French and Finish. I am Finish and French and a little bit Slovakian or maybe Slovenian, it's almost the same.

VOICE OF MAN WITH SMALL PENIS: Oh, Hungarian and Finish are related. They are non-Indo-European languages, but they are related to each other, isn't that funny? Sort of like links of primates that are not related to humans but are only related to each other. I love evolution and linguistics.

VOICE OF MAN WITH LARGE PENIS: How funny is that! And how cool you are French and Finish. Can you sing a Finish song? Cultures are kept through their songs.

> *Everybody laughs and Lina sings a song badly out of tune. There is applause. There is a brief silence.*

VOICE OF MAN WITH LARGE PENIS: Remember?

VOICE OF MAN WITH SMALL PENIS: Remember?

LINA's Voice: I remember when ....

MINA's Voice: I remember that ...

MINA and LINA's Voices: And now let's make children!

> *There is sound of laughter, songs, kisses, moans; shadows embracing are seen through the train windows. Then there are intergalactic sounds and flashing lights, the same as before, followed by profound silence.*

LINA's Voice: Oh, that was fun. These children will be Finish and Polish and a little bit Balkan. That will give them the spice, Balkan always adds spice.

MINA's Voice: I haven't had so much fun in ages. Since my mother dropped me on the way to the market. These children will be Hungarian and Lithuanian.

VOICE OF MAN WITH SMALL PENIS: What a miracle! A small penis can also produce babies, beautiful Hungarian Finish Balkan babies. Why have the men of our country waged the stupid civil war after all?

VOICE OF MAN WITH LARGE PENIS: Forget the war my friend, focus on this new beginning of international babies that we have created with the two most enticing, most exciting, most ethnographic women in the galaxy.

LINA's Voice: Remember?

MINA's Voice: I don't know, what do you remember?

LINA's Voice: Oh no, not memory again!

VOICE OF MAN WITH SMALL PENIS: Here goes another memory, catch it.

VOICE OF MAN WITH LARGE PENIS: Hold the baby. Hold the memory. The baby needs a memory of where she was born.

LINA and MINA's Voices: These babies were conceived and born on a train. The only place to be born. They were born in exile.

MEN'S Voices: Tell them the stories of their births so they remember.

GIRL ON THE FIRST PLANET: So, they remember! So, they don't forget how they were born, why and where they were born. And also, so that they can forget once in a while and then remember it in dreams and in memories and in letters written to their friends. Lina and Mina brought our planet back to life with their ingenuity, their songs and linguistic skills, their urban planning and their unafraid copulating skills. Long live Lina and Mina!

Sounds of babies laughing and cooing, then French music, then Hungarian music, Finish, Polish, laughter, voices, animated life. Clarinet and guitar music are heard as well.

All characters come back out on stage holding the babies they just made. Directorial imagination is needed to represent the babies.

MAN WITH SMALL PENIS: Let's do the tango now, the fandango, the flamenco, the rumba, the samba, the mambo, the mango, everybody. Let's renew the world with our renewed bodies and dances of the world with funny sounding names.

MAN WITH LARGE PENIS: Yes, let us reclaim our bodies through dance and massage therapy, small penis, big penis, vagina, clitoris, whatever! Let's start a complex world that is also simple and cares not about the form and shape of genitalia in the creation of its social structures.

MINA: I know, it's gross, right?

GIRL ON THE FIRST PLANET: So, are you going to marry each other?

LINA, MINA AND THE TWO MEN (*In unison with pathos and conviction*): Marriage? Never, Marriage is an old-fashioned obelisk, tower, column with no air to breathe no roundness to stretch and envelop. We are surprised by such an obsolete question on this newly revived planet.

GIRL ON THE FIRST PLANET: Pardon my clumsiness! I used marriage as a manner of speaking, the old language is obsolete for a new world. I will order a new language as well. We'll have to hire some professional linguists to create new languages for the new homes. Are you going to make homes of each other now?

MINA AND LINA: Home. I'll be your home, you'll be my home, mi casa tu casa, and we'll keep this as a potential home idea after we visit the other planets. Competition, competition! Bye-bye home! Bye-bye babies and bye-bye new round curvaceous cities we have created. We'll return, don't forget us, all right?

GIRL ON THE FIRST PLANET, THE TWO MEN AND THE BABIES *(The two men and Girl on the First Planet wave at Mina and Lina)*: Bye-bye Mina and Lina, don't forget us, remember you always have a home here, whenever you are tired of sleeping and traveling in your flower house, whenever you are tired of sleeping on the side of the road and living in exile, come back to us and enjoy our round city and our healthy bodies. Don't forget your children! You made them; YOU MADE THESE CHILDREN.

Intergalactic music again.

ACT II

The Second Planet – Eating the Landscapes We Yearn for

> *Intergalactic music continues throughout the stage directions. Mina and Lina wake up on the Second Planet inside their unfolding portable flower houses and come out of them sleepy and dazzled by the new landscapes. There are desert dunes with red flowers sprinkled all over them, mountains with snow-capped peaks in the distance; it all looks mysteriously and alluringly fresh, sparkling, and colorful.*

LINA: What kind of planet is this Mina? Look at the red flowers coming out of the desert, it all looks so yummy, I want to eat it. Maybe we have found our home. Maybe this is the planet where people eat their surroundings. No need to shop for food and cook. No need to worry about the antibiotics in the milk and the cheese. You just walk through the desert and eat red flowers. I'm tired of homeless. I'm tired of our stupid little folding and unfolding houses. I want a Balkan song. I want a place of my own that I can eat and where I can feel its sweet juices fill my mouth. I want my mama.

MINA: And then when you get tired of your edible landscapes and of the color of the desert and discover the reckless stupidity of the inhabitants and their wars, then you will beg me to start travelling again and to start looking for another home, another planet. And you'll cry your heart out when you have to pull your pretty little roots out of these desert dunes, and you'll wish you had never settled. You'll wish you were the tribe of Bedouins we once were. Remember?

LINA: Remember? What do you remember?

MINA: I remember walking through the desert with our tribe of Bedouins and our caravans and goats and jewels made from camel's teeth. Remember? What do you remember?

LINA: I remember the whistling of a train leaving a train station in a city by a sea somewhere in the Baltic region. Or was it the Balkan region? I remember walking through deserted streets on the way back from the train station and the whistling that followed me and my caravan of Gypsies with pigs and yellow skirts and copper jewelry as we were passing through a town where everybody had died. I want a place to call my own. I want my mama. _sense of heritage / community, familiarity_

MINA: You have such life affirming memories. That's why I don't believe in memory, it always brings you down, you either are nostalgic for that moment or you wish you had never experienced it, you either yearn for it or regret it. We have always been nomads, haven't we? We have been Bedouins and Gypsies, and travelers, we have always been walking, riding, crawling, swimming and running and then putting up our folding houses at night. We have always forgotten everything we remember. _Survival technique_

GIRL ON THE SECOND PLANET (*She is sitting on a colorful huge poufy silk cushion in the middle of the desert, surrounded by luscious red and yellow flowers and sparkling artesian fountains. She is talking to herself in a mirror as if rehearsing a part. She sees the two travelers, Mina and Lina and waves at them to come nearer, then places the mirror so that they can both see themselves in the mirror. Everything is luscious*): Oh, my goodness, we have visitors, how superior and delicious. We love visitors. Here look at yourselves in the mirror to see what you look like at the arrival on our planet. When you leave, you'll have to look again and then you'll see the difference. Do you know your parts, can we rehearse and then perform tonight?

LINA and MINA: What parts? What rehearsal? What performance? Are you the leader of this planet?

GIRL ON THE SECOND PLANET: Yes, I am the ultimate leader, not only of this planet but of the surrounding planets and properties. Here we play all the time; we rehearse and give performances. We keep our people happy and occupied by removing them from themselves through the roles of the world's best theater and opera repertoires. Want to see, want to stay? Want to be Clytemnestra, Achilles, Madonna, Iphigenia, Ophelia, Figaro, Mrs. Warren, Suzanna, the Devil, Ulysses, Tom Sawyer, Alice, Tom Jones, a young girl in love, an old woman in love, a boy on the run, a nun with a gun, a sailor, a traitor, a perpetrator, a saint, a savior, a flower?

LINA: Wow, how can you keep track of all that, don't you ever get dizzy? I don't know, we are looking for a home, for a new place to settle, we are tired of our many travels and would like to take a break from our nomadic lives for a while. Wouldn't this role playing be just another way of being nomadic? A nomadism of the mind? Plus, I can't remember a thing. I tend to forget all my parts if you know what I mean.

MINA: Speak for yourself Lina, you know how I feel about this issue of home, settling, roots, blah, blah, blah. I am looking for experience, for new homes that we can leave in search of other homes, for new roles that we can put on and take off like silk dresses, like butterflies.

LINA: We are looking for a place to create new memories.

MINA: We are looking for a place to forget.

GIRL ON THE SECOND PLANET: You can't forget, it's easier to remember. It's easier to live with your memories and stack them up like used books, they might come in handy at some point. In any case, I was once like you, in search of a new home, I was once living in that imperialist country the Planet America and I thought I was happy living there amidst ponderosa pines and dry gulches in the Wild West, a perpetual Western movie fantasy. Until one day when a man with a gun, when two men with guns, when a thousand men with guns ...... And I had had enough of the whole Western crap. I decided to emigrate and leave everything, ponderosa pines and all. But sometimes I miss it. Sometimes I yearn for it so badly I have to ride these bicycles over all the cliffs on the planet and concuss myself into oblivion. So, then I decided to do the constant theater thing, the playing of parts, of the world's best theater repertoires. It works, this is how we populated our country. We play and play until we forget our identities and yearnings. Want to join in, want to immigrate? There are many advantages, plus, here almost everything you see is edible, even the bicycles are edible. They are made of marzipan, and if you leave them in the sun they start melting and they are delicious.

MINA: It sounds like a great idea, but I don't know if my friend here would go for it. She is always yearning for something, a home, a Balkan song, her mama, a little hallway, a train whistle ... What do you say Lina, do you want to stay here for a while? Maybe if you try the whole playing of parts thing, you'll forget your yearnings and won't worry so much about a home, roots, or a place to settle. Remember?

LINA: I forgot. I don't remember. I was born in the air and I was born nowhere. I need to remember something; I need to have something to remember. A pond, a train station, a Balkan song. Let's stay here for a while and eat the landscapes, maybe I'll be cured and I'll be my own landscape and the need to remember will just pass, like some unwanted gas.

GIRL ON THE SECOND PLANET: Weren't you born somewhere?

LINA: I don't remember. I'm hungry.

>*Lina starts eating handfuls of the sand dunes, red flowers, marzipan bicycles, chewy and prickly cacti. Two men in white hospital gowns march over to Lina and Mina and arrest them. They force them to get into an old-fashioned buggy and they take them into a white room. Everything is white, shiny, transparent, and scary in its sterilized and sanitized cleanliness and whiteness.*

MEN IN WHITE GOWNS: You are therefore condemned to death by yearning. You have eaten our landscapes, you greedy bitches. How could you?

MINA: We are immigrants, we didn't know this was metaphorical, we don't understand the idiomatic expressions of this planet. Girl on Second Planet told us the landscapes were edible and we should just go ahead and take a bite. We thought it was literal. Yearning is literal, is in the guts. My friend here misses terribly having born somewhere and she thought she might quench some of that thirst with bits and pieces of your delicious landscape.

MEN IN WHITE GOWNS: Girl on Second Planet is an impostor, she knows nothing; she is an immigrant like you and has taken our jobs and our souls, and our ideas. You know the way immigrants always do. Now she poses as queen of the planet and goes about reciting her stupid parts from back home where she apparently was some big shot in a New York theater. If you ask me, I think she was deported, I think she must have crossed some illegal borders or some borders illegally and they found out. The Homeland Security deported her and sent her to our planet where she has taken our jobs, used our foods, and consumed our landscape. Die, die, die. You both have to die of punishment and of missing and of yearning. Serves you right, you female impostors, immigrant, illegal people, creatures, consumers!

MINA *(Pulls out a sword hidden beneath her cape and threatens to kill the Men in White Gowns)*: Shut up you self-important clowns, you are the impostor ones. Girl on Second Planet moved here to get away from the likes of you on Planet Earth, you immigrant women haters.

LINA AND GIRL ON SECOND PLANET: Go Mina, show them, yeah show them what you've got girl! Kill the stupid Men in White Gowns. Who wears those ridiculous outfits anyways, no sense of style and decorum? Kill them and rid the galaxy of immigrant haters, of women haters, of all haters.

MINA: On second thought I think I'll spare them. I don't want to live with their deaths on my conscience even though they richly deserve it. And by the way this was a Shakespearean rendition that I learned in acting school with sword fighting and all. It proves the point of Girl on Second Planet about how playing parts can save your life.

MAN IN WHITE GOWN 1(*He starts crying*): Don't kill us Mina, have pity on us Mina.

MAN IN WHITE GOWN 2: We'll try to learn tolerance and respect for immigrants, we promise.

MAN IN WHITE GOWN 1: What good would killing us do to you? Make us become your greatest fans.

MAN IN WHITE GOWN 2: Our parents were immigrants too, they came from Lithuania, but they always cursed immigrants of other races, so we learned hate too.

MAN IN WHITE GOWN 1: Immigrants can be racists too, you know, they can be intolerant of other immigrants.

MINA: Yeah, alright, whatever you stupid clowns, you are free to live. I'll put back my great grandfather's sword that he used in the civil war of nineteen something and that Hamlet used when he killed Polonius behind the curtain. And you've got a point there about immigrants also being racist and full of prejudices. That's why unlike my beautiful sentimental partner here I think we should do away with the notion of home and forget about birth, native this and native that and chose exile. Chose living on the road and eating the landscape.

LINA: That's right, you said it girlfriend! I'm so hungry. And yet I can't help it. I'm hungry for home, I'm hungry for dirt, for earth dirt, birth dirt, native dirt. All this exile stuff is crap. I'm going to eat everything. I'll eat everybody. I'll eat you all until I have a home. I'll be a big fat pregnant Goddess of the universe. I'll eat everything in sight but mostly human flesh. There Girl on Second Planet, this is my big role, my big part to end all Hollywood and Broadway parts: Lina the Minotaur Girl. That's what happens when you lose your home, and nobody fucking believes you about how badly that hurts.

> *Lina starts eating everything she sees around her, she chomps on the two men, she eats flowers and whole pieces of landscape, she even bites Mina until Girl of First Planet. Men in White Gown's administer a calming injection. Wild music while she's eating everything, threatening, ominous, horror film treatment.*

ACT III

The Third Planet: Snow Planet, Snow White

> *Music plays under stage directions. Lina and Mina travel again in their spaceships. They reach the planet of the Woman Who Eats Hearts. The planet is all white, covered in sparkling snow. On the expanse of snow there are throbbing human hearts that writhe, cry, sing and talk. They live just like miniature human beings. Other creatures move across the snow or freeze in a pose. They are ghosts of devoured travelers.*

WOMAN WHO EATS HEARTS *(Laughing in a low voice, witch like but also in an alluring way):* Hello my dearies, what brings you to my planet? It's so late in the day, I was getting ready for a nap, but now that I have visitors, I'll just put that off. I always have time for new visitors.

MINA*(Cunningly)*: Hello Woman Who Eats Hearts. We have heard of your planet all the way from Planet Earth and after traveling to a couple of other sorry planets, we decided to visit you as well for our research project.

LINA *(Trying to be cunning like Mina, but still sort of fragile and shaky from the visit of the previous planet)*: Yea, that's right Woman Who Eats Hearts, your fame has travelled through all the galaxies and we are curious to find out the secrets of your planet, how it works, how you manage to keep the snow so white and sparkling all the time and the standard of living of your inhabitants so elevated?

WOMAN WHO EATS HEARTS: Are you trying to flatter me, so you escape my wrath? It never works, they've all tried, and look there at all the whining poor little hearts waiting to be cooked up in a nice juicy stew later today.

MINA: Not so fast, Woman Who Eats Hearts, you might just have found your match. Here I introduce you to Lina, Cina, Bobina, the Minotaur Girl. She's just had a feast of hearts and livers and entire settlements in the country of the Girl on Second Planet. An entire army of Men in White Gowns had to put her down with special injections or she would have completely devoured the planet. You'd better beware, this is one hungry raging Minotauress.

WOMAN WHO EATS HEARTS: Is that so? We'll see. The first test you have to pass in order to convince me not to eat your hearts, is to cross the field yonder there, listen to all the pathetic stories that all the slimy hearts and creatures have to tell and make it back without one tear shed, one step faltering, ready to rule.

LINA: Rule what?

MINA: Yea, what and who are we supposed to rule?

WOMAN WHO EATS HEARTS: Don't contradict me, just do what I say. When you rule, you rule, there's no what, there's no who, you just fucking rule, you stupid bitches. Ha, Minotaur Girl, that's a good joke if I ever heard one.

LINA(*Trying to be cunning again, winking at Mina as if to suggest that they need to just go along with whatever the Woman says*): All right, all right, we got it, no need to get all worked out about it. (*Then whispering to Mina*): I think we can con her, she's voracious and fierce, but ignorant and not very smart. I don't think this planet is for us and it's better off destroyed (*Mina and Lina laugh in a conspiratorial manner*).

MINA: All Right Woman Who Eats Hearts, please give us a chance to prove ourselves on this hideous planet of yours and see if we can earn the white of these snows and if we do, you're history, we get to eat your heart, deal? Or all right, I'm not much into heart eating, but my girlfriend here sort of acquired a real taste for it recently, as a result of utmost yearning for home or something tacky like that.

WOMAN WHO EATS HEARTS (*Rubbing her hands with witch-like satisfaction*): Understood my dearies, let's see who eats whose heart in the end.

> *Mina and Lina start walking across the white expanse of snow. The hearts sprinkled onto this expanse tell wrenching stories of abandonment and perdition. Snow music.*

CHORUS OF HEARTS MEMBER 1: I left my home and my children in a dark deep ditch with cold water back home, back home in a Balkan country. I left for a better life, for greener pastures and whiter snows, but now I want to be back in the cold ditch with my two baby boys. They are probably dead; everything is dead and cold and ditch in the Balkans.

CHORUS OF HEARTS MEMBER 2: My country was at war; neighbors were killing neighbors and neighbors were raping neighbors. There was a red poppy flower in the middle of a blue pond. They put us on a bus and told us everything was going to be all right. The soldier who forced us on the bus kept telling us we were all going to be all right, all right, in the middle of a blue pond, in the middle of a field of poppies and red carnations. We all drowned and were covered in red poppy water.

CHORUS OF HEARTS MEMBER 3: I wasn't too unhappy in my country, but I left it because everybody was leaving it. Some left it for a new leather jacket, others left it for the freedom of speech blah, blah and others left it because they couldn't stand the stench. It stinks in the Balkans. I would give everything to have a home, even in America. I heard in America you can live in mobile homes that are transported on trucks and placed in the middle of a field next to other mobile homes. You can even have a vegetable garden in the back of the mobile home. And when you don't like the surroundings of your mobile home anymore you can take your home on a big truck and move it in a nicer place, next to a nice smelling mountain for instance.

CHORUS OF HEARTS MEMBER 4: Mamas, mamas, look at me, take me out of here, please take me back with you. Remember me? I'm your son.

> *Mina and Lina both stop horrified, look at each other, look at the speaking heart, fall on their knees embracing each other and sobbing.*

CHORUS OF HEARTS MEMBER 4: Mamas, mamas, take me out of here, please. The Woman Who Eats Hearts is going to eat me. I'll be a good boy from now on, I won't do drugs. I won't even smoke cigarettes. I won't steal and cheat. I'll get a job and live happily ever after.

MINA: How could we forget we had a son, Lina?

LINA: How could we forget we had a son, Mina?

MINA: Remember, remember, remember...

LINA: Forget, forget, forget!

MINA: We left home...

LINA: We forgot everything, but everything didn't forget us.

CHORUS OF HEARTS: Stand up Mina and Lina, pretend, pretend, pretend, or the Woman Who Eats Hearts will eat your son that you forgot about.

CHORUS OF HEARTS MEMBER 4: Mamas, mamas, mamas, I'll be a good boy, take me out of this snow. I'm cold and don't have a shirt, my heart is freezing. You must find the rest of my body; she puts the bodies in a cupboard at the end of the snowy field. My body is in the drawer that says: "bad boys who do drugs." It's a green drawer. Please mamas, put my body and heart together and I'll be a good boy until happily ever after and I'll never do drugs again and I'll take care of you when you are old and tired.

WOMAN WHO EATS HEARTS: Just you wait, you intergalactic bitches. Either of you cries or prays or any of that sentimental crap and you are history. Here is my special de-hearting machine waiting to be used on you and there is the empty cupboard waiting to be filled with your nice juicy bodies.

MINA: I was wrong all along, Lina, we need a home that is not exile, we need a place where we can grow roots and bake potatoes and plant a lilac tree that smells like a corner of our childhood in a dictatorial country where we once lived. Let's save our son from Woman Who Eats Hearts and go home.

CHORUS OF HEARTS MEMBER 4: Yes, let's go home mamas, if not she'll eat my heart or worse still, sell my heart back to organ thieves from Bulgaria. Get my body from the cupboard and let's run.

MINA: All right, what are we waiting for now that we're awake again? I'll do a fake forgetfulness phony happiness dance that Woman Who Eats Hearts will take for real because even though she's fierce and greedy, she's also ignorant and stupid and racist.

LINA: A fake forgetfulness phony happiness dance? What the fuck are you talking about?

MINA: I know what I'm talking about, I'm an actress, I can do it. I can pretend, remember?

LINA: I thought we agreed I had a real problem remembering anything. I forgot we had a son, why would I remember that you are an actress? Besides if you are in a pretend mode all the time that would prevent me from remembering anything real about you because you'd always be playing a role, right? Who are you Mina, really, other than the other mother of our son here divided into heart and body on this gruesome freezing planet?

MINA: Don't you worry, you just take my lead for now and you'll find out who I really am later when we have the time for that kind of psychoanalytic nonsense. I'll do all the acting while you just stay still and don't act. Protect our son here, protect his heart and when I wink at you, run to the cupboard and take his body out of the drawer. You understand spatial relations better than I do, right? Our professions should be of some use to us now. Why did we ever get those fucking PhD's if we can't even get away from a heart eating witch and save our son from being sold to organ thieves from Bulgaria?

> *Music through the stage directions. Mina does the tree dance, swaying in the wind. There are no trees on the planet, on the entire expanse of snow, so Woman Who Eats Hearts is captured by the dance while also repulsed. Then Mina begins a silent dance in which she rounds herself up trying to look like a cloud. This is the cloud dance. Woman Who Eats Hearts is repulsed and appalled by Mina's acting, dancing, and cloud concoction. In the meantime, Lina moves towards a green shiny dresser with huge drawers like those in a morgue. One of the drawers holds her son's body.*

LINA (*Quietly, mouthing the words in an exaggerated way*): What's his name?

MINA (*Also quietly*): What?

LINA: What's his name? The name of the child?

MINA (*Quietly, with silent stress on every syllable*): I don't know.

CHORUS OF HEARTS MEMBER 4: My name is Billy, mamas! Billy, like in Billy goat.

> *A colorful garden appears. A little boy in a sailor's outfit is playing with boats in a little pond in the middle of the garden. Two women who look like younger versions of Mina and Lina are sitting in wicker chairs reading a book and looking over the book occasionally at the boy, with love and then smiling at each other contentedly. The music is happy, beautiful, light, joyful.*

BILLY: Mamas, look, look, I can make the boat float, it's floating, it's moving. It's going to China.

YOUNG LINA AND MINA: That's wonderful sweetie. So proud of you! Billy, sweet Billy our dear Billy goat.

BILLY: Mamas, why do boats float?

LINA: Because they have to take people from one shore to the other. They are a means of transportation. They go to China.

MINA (*Laughing with endearment*): Oh, listen to the urban planner in you. Boats also float because they add fluid beauty to the world, because it's more fun to float than to walk or drive. And because they must save Ophelia.

BILLY: Who is Ophelia mamas?

MINA AND LINA: Ophelia is, Ophelia was a girl who ....

> *Warlike, cannon shots, explosions. Frightening sounds of shooting and cannons are heard and soldiers with machine guns enter the garden, ravaging and destroying*

everything in sight, taking Billy and perpetrating great violence on the two women. A secret door opens revealing a dingy dungeony room with metal chairs, a table and a metal bed with a filthy mattress. Younger versions of Mina and Lina, yet older than in the garden scene are each tied to a chair while men with torture instruments are moving back and forth.

BULGARIAN ORGAN THIEF 1: You tell us where you hid your creep of a son or we'll carve out your little kidneys and livers like you carve a pig for Christmas.

BULGARIAN ORGAN THIEF 2: Yea, that's right you bitches, we can get ten grand for a kidney these days and the double of that for a liver. They're in high demand.

MINA AND LINA: We don't know. *(Sounds of hitting and torture in the dark. Sounds of both younger and older Mina and Lina crying and begging for mercy are also heard)*. We don't know, we would tell you if we knew. He was taken away from us. You should know.

BULGARIAN ORGAN THIEF 1: What did you say, you stupid cunts? Do you know how much a heart sells for these days? The heart of a Croatian traitor cunt?

BULGARIAN ORGAN THIEF 2: Fifty grand, that's how much. We could make more money selling your filthy Croatian hearts to American mafia than selling your little prick of a boy.

BULGARIAN ORGAN THIEF 1: Yes, we are kind and compassionate, aren't we Kolya? We are kind and compassionate men who want to save you and sell your dick of a son to an American family who would give him a good life with toy trucks and Lego toys.

BULGARIAN ORGAN THIEF 2: And with soccer balls and a nice American soccer mom who drives a minivan. That's what we would give your weasel of a Croatian mother fucking son.

MINA: We don't know where our son is, so kill us.

LINA: Yes, so kill us, take out our hearts, livers, kidneys and sell them to the American mafia and to a soccer mom. Tell us if you find our son, we've been looking for him too.

MINA: Yes, tell us if you find our son.

> *Lina and Mina are lying on the floor at the end of the scene. Then the secret door closes and the image of the dungeony room disappears. We are back on the expanse of the snowy field.*

MINA: Now I know everything. There was a war.

LINA: There was a war and we barely escaped.

MINA: Like a miracle.

LINA: I wish I had never remembered.

MINA: I wish we were still in the garden.

LINA: It was a happy time. What came after ...

MINA: Don't talk about it, now we need to forget again. *better to forget or remember?*

LINA: Start over as they say ...

MINA: Yes, start over ... Who says that?

MINA: Are we already dead Lina?

LINA: I don't know, maybe not. We'll just have to wait and see.

- 49 -

BILLY: You are not dead mamas since you travelled all the way here to this planet to save me. You did travel all this way to save me, right?

MINA (*looking confused, disconcerted, not knowing what to say*): Yea, sure sweetie, of course...

LINA: ... we travelled all the way here looking for you.

MINA: Are we Croatian?

LINA: I don't know, I thought I was Finish and you were Polish.

MINA: I thought you were French, and I was Hungarian.

LINA: Was there a war?

MINA: I think so. A Balkan war.

LINA: Was it Bosnia, Serbia, Croatia, Slovenia?

MINA: Or was it Slovakia, Montenegro, Macedonia?

LINA: Romania, Bulgaria, Latvia?

MINA: Was it Balkania?

LINA: Was it Blinia?

MINA: I think it was Blinia. There are always wars in that part of the world. They fought over Blinis, cheese, potato, and marmalade Blinis. That's why the war started.

LINA: That's why the war started.

MINA: In another country it started because of the penis size.

LINA: I know, right! We made babies with the last two men left on the planet. Our babies should be grown children by now. We have so many children and that's why we forget about them.

MINA: That was fun.

LINA: Yes, that was fun. Riding the train and making babies while singing French music was fun.

BILLY: Mamas, mamas, I am freezing here in the snow, hurry up please and remember your lives later. Get my body out of the drawer, please, or my heart will disintegrate and won't fit my body anymore. Remember, the drawer that says: "bad boys who do drugs."

MINA: Why are you in the drawer for "bad boys who do drugs?" We didn't raise you that way.

LINA: Yea, that's right, we raised you with sailing boats and fairy tales, in a beautiful garden in a Balkan country before the war during a brief spell of peace.

BILLY: I know, you were good mamas, but you only raised me to the age of six. Then the war came, and I was kidnapped, remember? I was raised by Bulgarian Organ Thieves and then sold to an alcoholic soccer mom and later put in foster care in an American city on planet America. That's how I started using drugs, mamas. I swear, the kids in foster care all did it, so we all did it because it made us feel better when we were so sad and so lonely after we had been taken away from our parents.

> *Another secret door is opening, and we can see a city street with homeless people, drug dealers, sex workers and pimps and drug addicts looking for a quick fix. Billy as a teenager is staggering and buying drugs from a dealer.*

BILLY (*Talking to the dealer in a pleading, desperate manner*): I know, I know I haven't paid for the last time, I promise I'll give you the dough by tomorrow, please man give me a break. I have some dough coming tonight, just this one time man, what the fuck. (*The drug dealer kicks him and leaves him on the ground. Billy is crying and moaning.*) Why was I ever born, where are my mamas? I once had two pretty mamas who took care of me in a pretty garden and I was happy before the war and before the BULGARIAN ORGAN THIEVES. Why am I still alive? I wonder if my mamas are still alive! What wouldn't I give to be with them in a warm cozy home somewhere on a peaceful drug free planet with no soccer moms and no foster homes?

> *The Woman Who Eats Hearts appears and gives the drug dealer money. He exchanges Billy for a stash of cash and the Woman Who Eats Hearts runs away carrying him like a baby. The secret door closes and we are back on the white planet.*

MINA and LINA (*They both cry with large desperate grimaced silent cries, saying the lines a bit separate, not synchronized, but as if echoing one another*): Billy, sweet Billy, we are so sorry for everything, for being born and giving birth to you in a Balkan country that started a bad, bad war and then was overtaken by Bulgarian Organ Thieves. We didn't mean to. We should have known better. No wonder we forgot everything. No wonder we have been rambling like some interplanetary ghosts all over the universe.

> *Lina is sneaking up to the cupboard and is opening the drawer that contains Billy's body. Mina is distracting the Woman Who Eats Hearts with jittery motions.*

MINA (*Catching on Lina's game and going along in order to gain more time*): Are we Gypsies?

LINA: Are we Bulgarian?

MINA: Are we Aromani?

LINA: Do you think maybe we're Bunjevci?

MINA: Are we dead?

LINA: So many people in the Balkans and they all want to get along and have friendly wars.

MINA: Just like we get along.

LINA: Exactly the way we get along.

> *Lina finds Billy's body, pulls it out of the drawer with a quick move and everything goes blindingly white then blindingly black. There should be great and shocking contrasts of lighting. Whispers in the dark. Billy is heard laughing. Lina and Mina are heard laughing. Lights go back up, the landscape is no longer white, but multicolored.*

WOMAN WHO EATS HEARTS (*She is caught by seizures of rage*): You bitches, vipers, Balkan darkies, Balkan dykes, I should have known you, you, you, ay, ay, ay curses on you and your filthy cunts and your creep of a child, I once had a child, I ate it, I had ten children and ate them all, I once was a man and ate him, I once was a woman and ate her, vomit on you and your filthy multiculturalism. I once was head of state, mother fucking head of state in Indochina, then the war came, then another war came, then I started ethnic cleansing, too many races instead of just one, too many colors instead of just one, ethnic cleansing felt good, such a relief, all was going well on the planet and I had many juicy hearts waiting to be eaten, fuck, shit, cunt, ethnic cleansing, long live genocide, die, die, die.

The Woman Who Eats Hearts dissolves and disappears and where she once stood there is only a white puddle as if from the melting of a snow man. Snow melting sounds.

LINA: Oh, yikes the Woman Who Eats Hearts spoiled winter and snowmen for me forever.

BILLY (*Who is now a handsome young man*): Don't worry mamas, we are all together again like we once were in the garden before the war. I'll restore all the seasons for you: winter, spring, fall and summer. Right? We'll go to the country that has all the seasons. And we'll make snowmen and snowwomen in the winter that won't look anything like the Woman Who Eats Hearts. The witch is gone.

MINA: All the seasons: winter summer November May seaside, mountainside, downtown, marmalade and eggplant stew. We'll have everything and write it all over again. Your mother Lina will be the urban planner.

LINA: And your mother Mina will make dances in all colors and clouds and delicious marmalade like we used to eat in the Balkan garden during the six years of peace and motherhood. I no longer feel the need to eat the landscape. I think I'm cured of Minotaur Girl syndrome, maybe it was just the existence of the Woman Who Eats Hearts in the universe and her poisonous toxins that were making me so voracious.

> *All the hearts roaming the white expanse of snow now turn multicolor. They find their bodies and prepare for a celebratory dance.*

CHORUS OF HEARTS (*Dancing an animated rhythmic dance while singing. Thumping music for this scene*):

We are all heart and no nonsense

We hate it when people suffer from absence

We suffered enough in the cold and the snow

We were all kidnapped by organ thieves ten years ago

But Mina and Lina with good acting saved the day

And now our planet is like the month of May.

Goodbye Mina, Lina and sweet Billy boy

Don't forget us, it's hard to let go

Come back to visit because we love you so

Our home is your home, our heart is your heart

And we'll always remember that we all played a part

In killing the bad witch with cunning and art

We are no nonsense and all heart.

ACT IV – PLANET AMERICA

Theme song intergalactic music. The location is that of a large tent in the middle of desolate land, with people of various nationalities, races and ethnicities waiting to be called for interviews, papers, green cards, documents of their legal or illegal status on Planet America. There are children running around, old people dozing off, and several officers walking among them with machine guns. Everything is gray and shabby; the tent is almost falling apart and has huge holes in it through which gusts of wind and dust are at time blowing through.

BILLY: How much longer do we have to wait in this place, mamas? I'm so hungry.

LINA: It takes forever, doesn't it! Maybe it was a big mistake to come here.

MINA: What do you mean *here?* Here to this bloody immigration office tent or *here* to this ridiculous country, planet?

LINA: Both. Everything is so drab and colorless. And the cops with their big ass machine guns freak me out. They remind me of, of, you know ... I wish I was home.

MINA (*Staring at her in disbelief):* Home? You're kidding, right? Where is home? Did we ever have a home? We ran away from fucking home because of a war, remember?

BILLY: We did, we did, don't you remember? We were once a family and we had a home with a garden before ...

LINA: Oh, forget it, let's not talk about the past any longer, let's just look to the future! We are here now. It is what it is, and we'll wait our turn just like all these other good people here.

MINA: Since when are you so reconciliatory?

LINA: Since now. And since when do you use such ridiculous enormous words?

MINA: Since now. New words as long as a long day's night.

BILLY: Oh mamas, please don't argue now. We escaped so many, so many ...

MINA and LINA: Shhhhhhhh! Don't mention it. Don't talk about the past.

BILLY (*Taken aback by his mothers' suddenly stern attitude*): All right, all right mamas whatever! I'll be a good boy and won't talk about the past ... even though I really want to.

> *The Girl on First Planet is now Guatemalan Massage Therapist who is also waiting for her immigration interview or papers. The Man with Small Penis is Taxi Driver from Uzbekistan. The Man with Large Penis is Immigration Irritated Officer. The Woman Who Eats Hearts is now Very White Hitler Loving Woman.*

IRRITATED IMMIGRATION OFFICER:
Obradovskapopovicimanton family. Is this a real name you people? How can you get through life with such a name?

MINA, LINA, BILLY: Yes, here we are. That's right here we all are. The Obradovskapopovicimanton family. *Caricature of American? non-American of American names.*

IRRITATED IMMIGRATION OFFICER: Hum, let's see, papers!

LINA: Papers? What papers? We've come here for papers.

IRRITATED IMMIGRATION OFFICER: Immigration papers you stupid dykes.

MINA and LINA: What did you say?

IRRITATED IMMIGRATION OFFICER: You heard me.

MINA and LINA: No, we haven't heard you. Please repeat.

IRRITATED IMMIGRATION OFFICER: All right then (*Shouting so that everybody hears.*) The immigration papers you stupid dykes.

> *Everybody turns and stares at Lina and Mina at the same time almost in unison.*

IRRITATED IMMIGRATION OFFICER: Did you hear me now?

VERY WHITE HITLER LOVING WOMAN: Oh, here you are dearies! It's a small universe indeed. Pleased to meet your acquaintance again. Ha, ha, ha ...

IRRITTED IMMIGRATION CLERK (*Screaming at Very White Hitler Loving Woman*): Wait for your turn, you cow! Who said you could talk?

VERY WHITE HITLER LOVING WOMAN: *I* said I could talk, and Mr. Hitler said I could talk you piece of brown shit. And by the way these women are wanted on several planets.

IRRITATED IMMIGRATION OFFICER: What, where, how? What planets? What women? Why are they wanted?

VERY WHITE HITLER LOVING WOMAN: Exilic disobedience.

IRRITATED IMMIGRATION OFFICER: And what else?

VERY WHITE HITLER LOVING WOMAN: And escape with intent to never return!

IRRITATED IMMIGRATION OFFICER: Oooohh my! And what else, tell us Very White Hitler Loving Woman.

VERY WHITE HITLER LOVING WOMAN: And yearning for home and eating the landscape.

IRRITATED IMMIGRATION OFFICER: Oh my, what horror, what outrage! To death, to death, to death!

VERY WHITE HITLER LOVING WOMAN: And architectural feminism vandalism as part of urban planning and planet regeneration. Copulating in a train and making brown babies. And for saving hearts and bodies from the secret drawer!

IRRITATED IMMIGRATION OFFICER: Oh my, what horror, saving hearts, eating the landscape, making brown babies! To death, to death, to cruel and painful death.

> *The Irritated Immigration Officer backs Mina and Lina and Billy into a wall with his gun. Lina, Mina and Billy look terrified.*

VERY WHITE HITLER LOVING WOMAN: But first you are deported.

IRRITTED IMMIGRATION OFFICER: First you are deported and second you are executed on the border. To give a lesson to all those who cross the border and yearn, and vandalize, urban plan and make babies on trains and escape and escape ... Our borders must be safe, we have to secure our borders, our cities, our homes and our drawers. You can't be safe anywhere no more these days because of you scum immigrant people with no papers, with no papers and obscene names. Obscene names!

VERY WHITE HITLER LOVING WOMAN: To death with you, first we kill you and then we deport you, first we deport you and then we kill you, call the INS, call the IRS, call the CIA, the KGB, the BBC, the KKK, the NSA, the SSA, the ABC.

GUATEMALAN MASSAGE THERAPIST: Wait a minute, aren't these Mina and Lina?

TAXI DRIVER FROM UZBEKISTAN: That's right, it is our dears Mina and Lina. Your babies are all grown now, they are populating the world and traveling in space in search of a peaceful planet. I am sorry to say, but our planet was almost destroyed by drones from Planet America. But we had a good life while it lasted.

GUATEMALAN MASSAGE THERAPIST: And we saved the babies.

DRIVER FROM UZBEKISTAN: All of them. And sent them into space.

GUATEMALAN MASSAGE THERAPIST: But now we must save Mina and Lina and Billy. Let's riot and let's take down this evil place. Let's save this planet from immigration officers and spineless clerks and organ traffickers.

IRRITATED IMMIGRATION OFFICER: You are doing nothing of the sort you evil bitches and limp dicks. You are going to prison and to concentration camp for a thousand years.

> *Irritated Immigration Officer pulls out a machine gun and points it at Lina, Mina, Billy and at all the immigrants who are defending them.*

IRRITATED IMMIGRATION OFFICER: All right, nobody moves, or I'll blast all your stupid illegal immigrant brains out right here right now. Go over there against that wall and don't any of you dare move or I'll shoot the fuck out of your sorry refugee selves.

GUATEMALAN MASSAGE THERAPIST (*Timidly raising her hand as if wanting to say something very politely*): Can I give you all a massage first Mister Irritated Immigration Officer?

IRRITATED IMMIGRATION OFFICER: What? What did you just say, you stupid Hispanic cow?

GUATEMALAN MASSAGE THERAPIST: Hey no need to be so rude. You are going to shoot us anyways, aren't you? Give us a chance. Let me give you a massage. It will feel good and it will relax you before you kill us all.

VERY WHITE HITLER LOVING WOMAN: Hey, I'd like a massage. My back has been killing me for centuries. I could really use a massage. Let's give the bitches a chance, alright?

IRRITATED IMMIGRATION OFFICER: What? What did you say Very White Hitler Loving Woman? Have you lost your mind, are you taking their defense?

VERY WHITE HITLER LOVING WOMAN: Far be it from me, I hate the bitches and their whiny offspring as much as any of you here. But why not take advantage of their skills first before we kill them? *profit off of labor of immigrants, barely pay them*

IRRITATED IMMIGRATION OFFICER and VERY WHITE HITLER LOVING WOMAN: Hmm, ah, ooh, good point! Why not, why not, why not! Take advantage first and kill them afterwards. Why not, why not, why not! Why yes, why yes, why yes!

GUATEMALAN MASSAGE THERAPIST: I will give you the Guatemalan massage from Quetzaltenango. It is a bubbly and bombastic massage. It makes you want to live at home and remember your childhood. It makes you want to ride a wild horse. We eat *aliote* and *chiote* in Guatemala. It has been handed down to me from my great uncle Almadivo ...

IRRITATED IMMIGRATION OFFICER and VERY WHITE HITLER LOVING WOMAN: We don't want to hear about your asshole uncle Alvo calvo whatever ...

VERY WHITE HITLER LOVING WOMAN: Start your massages and stop the lecturing if you want to stay alive another hour.

IRRITATED IMMIGRATION OFFICER: Yes, start massaging if you want to stay alive for one more hour.

VERY WHITE HITLER LOVING WOMAN (*Laughing wickedly and greedily*): And then we kill them and cook them.

IRRITATED IMMIGRATION OFFICER and VERY WHITE HITLER LOVING WOMAN (*With a rhythmic beat sounding like an ominous chant*): We kill them and cook them. We bake them and fry them. Yum, yum!

VERY WHITE HITLER LOVING WOMAN: We marinate them in vinegar and oil. Yum, yum!

IRRITATED IMMIGRATION OFFICER: Then we boil and fry and bake them in red curry. Yum, yum!

The chant has to become terrifying and demented.

GUATEMALAN MASSAGE THERAPIST (*Suddenly shouting in an overpowering voice that covers everybody else's voices*): Get on the tables, you cowardly disjointed haters.

Guatemalan Massage Therapist is holding a semi-automatic pointed at the clerks and policemen and at Very White Hitler Loving Woman that she was able to pull out of the pocket of her dress in a moment of inattention of the assailants.

MINA (*holds a hunting rifle*): Yea, let's see who's going to eat who.

LINA (*Pulls out a sword from the civil war*): Who is going to eat whom!

GUATEMALAN MASSAGE THERAPIST (*In rhythm that starts to sound like a chant matching the previous chant of the clerks and policemen, only more upbeat and livelier*): Whom, whom, whom! Who is going to eat whom! Yum, yum. Whom, whom, yum, yum, whom, whom, yum, yum.

> *Irritated Immigration Officer and Very White Hitler Loving Woman tremble and they climb on the long conference tables in the immigration tent, face down prepared for massages.*

GUATEMALAN MASSAGE THERAPIST: Just look at this. What have we here? Bodies, bodies, bodies! Tired, disjointed, abused, unused, badly used, overused, underused, angry, inflatable, deflectable bodies. No wonder you all are so fucked up in your heads. *abused by capitalism, fear losing their shitty jobs*

> *She gets up on one of the tables and starts walking and running over the bodies while also performing massaging. She gathers Lina, Mina, Billy, Taxi Driver from Uzbekistan around her and gives them instructions about how to massage everybody else.*

IRRITATED IMMIGRATION OFFICER and VERY WHITE HITLER LOVING WOMAN: More, more, more! More, more, more! Don't stop, don't ever stop, massage us till we die.

GUATEMALAN MASSAGE THERAPIST (*She shouts in the same army-like manner*): Shut up, face down, relax! Shut up, eyes closed, relax!

MINA, LINA, BILLY, TAXI DRIVER FROM UZBEKISTAN (*In rhythmic cadence*): Shut up, face down, relax! Shut up, eyes closed, relax! Breathe in, breathe out, breathe in, breathe out, shut up!

GUATEMALAN MASSAGE THERAPIST: Breathe in, breathe out, shut up! Breathe in, breathe out, shut up!

LINA: Let's see if we can save this planet and make it our home.

MINA: Oh you, and your home obsession.

BILLY: She's right, mama. We need a home. I want to say I'm going home. All my friends in school can say that, only I can't because I have no idea what our home is.

GUATEMALAN MASSAGE THERAPIST: Homeless sort of sucks, your kid is right. I'd rather be homeful than homeless.

> *Guatemalan Massage Therapist, Taxi Driver from Uzbekistan, Mina, Lina, Billy, all massage the people stretched out on the tables with large movements, with their hands, fists, elbows, knees. Lina starts telling a story as she is performing a massage on one or several of the bodies.*

LINA: Once upon a time there was a girl from Blinia that was born by the side of the road.

MINA (*From now on the stories overlap, echo and interrupt one another. Mina is also massaging one or more bodies while talking*): Once upon a time there was a girl with a Lambanian mother who was born on the border with Lugubria ...

GUATEMALAN MASSAGE THERAPIST (*Talking and messaging*): But one day the country of Blinia started a war against their neighbors because they didn't like the way they planted their potatoes.

BILLY: And the country of Lugubria started a fierce persecution against women of the border so the girl with the Lambanian mother had to leave her home.

TAXI DRIVER FROM UZBEKISTAN: So, the Blinian girl had to start walking in search of another home. She was walking and crying and walking and crying ...

IRRITATED IMMIGRATION OFFICER: And what else? What happened?

VERY WHITE HITLER LOVING WOMAN: What happens next? Tell us!

MINA: The Lambanian girl was so hungry and she ran in the direction of a loud song and the smell of potato dumplings ....

LINA: And the Blinian girl was also very hungry and smelled a cactus stew fragrance, so she ran through the forest and ran and ran until ...

GUATEMALAN MASSAGE THERAPIST: She ran, and she ran, and she ran ... panting and singing ...

TAXI DRIVER FROM UZBEKISTAN: She ran, and she ran, and she ran panting and singing louder and louder ...

BILLY: Until the Lambanian girl bumped right into ....

TAXI DRIVER FROM UZBEKISTAN: Until the Blinian girl bumped right into ...

LINA: And one of the hungry girls said to the other hungry girl:

MINA: Where are you from?

LINA: I'm from the side of the road in Blinia but I ran away. Where are you from?

MINA: I am Lambanian by mother but was born on the border with Lugubria. I also ran away.

LINA: Cool, do you want to get married and live happily ever after?

MINA: Totally. Let's get married right away.

LINA: Here in the forest?

MINA: Yes, here in the forest.

LINA: Who is going to marry us?

MINA: Hum, good question.

BILLY: At that same exact moment, a wood cutter who was also a marriage counselor happened to be passing by and overhearing their conversation offered to marry them right there on the spot.

LINA: Now that we are married let's eat.

MINA: Yes, let's eat your potato dumplings.

LINA: Yes, let's eat your cactus stew.

MINA: Now that we ate let's make a baby.

LINA: Yes, you're right, I sort of like having a baby too.

MINA: But how do you make a baby?

LINA: You kiss, and you kiss, and you get naked with each other and then you have a baby.

GUATEMALAN MASSAGE THERAPIST: So they got naked with each other and they kissed and they fell asleep in each other's arms and the next morning they saw a beautiful baby boy sleeping between them in the forest on the bed of pine cones and leaves that the kind marriage counselor had built for them as a wedding gift. They cuddled and kissed the baby and fed him milk from their nipples and decided they needed to get going and find a home for their new family.

BILLY: And they visited many wondrous planets and achieved many valiant deeds. And they saved the heart of their son and made him one with his body again and melted the Woman Who Eats Hearts to a tiny puddle.

> *The two evil characters on the tables are sleeping blissfully. Mina, Lina, Billy, Guatemalan Massage Therapist and Taxi Driver from Uzbekistan stop the massages.*

GUATEMALAN MASSAGE THERAPIST: Shhh, let's get out of here now before they wake up.

MINA: Where are we going?

LINA: We are going home. Some version of home, somewhere we want to keep coming back to and that we want to remember.

BILLY: Won't they come after us in the morning and kill us mamas?

TAXI DRIVER FROM UZBEKISTAN: Don't worry Billy, I used a special potion from Ougadougou on their bodies and when they wake up, they will all feel like yearning refugees and hopefully they will be kinder and sorry for everything they did.

GUATEMALAN MASSAGE THERAPIST: Yea, me too I used Aunt Juanita's special potion for consciousness awareness.

- 67 -

make them acknowledge themselves

They will remember their evil deeds and will be punished by helping yearning refugees resettle and immigrate for the rest of their lives. And they'll be organ donors, too.

TAXI DRIVER FROM UZBEKISTAN: The planets will be realigned. Bodies and hearts will be reunited on all the planets.

GUATEMALAN MASSAGE THERAPIST: Yea, good job everybody. We are the new Scheherazades. Story tellers and massage therapists in one. We put disjointed bodies back in shape and twisted hearts back in rhythm. We buy time, we save our lives, one day at a time, one story at a time, one heart at a time. We'll never be unemployed.

TAXI DRIVER FROM UZBEKISTAN: That should get us work permits and legal status if anything ever will.

> *Everybody laughs and giggles quietly. Suddenly Mina and Lina are enveloped in a special warm light like an aura that makes them look ethereal, unearthly. Melodious music in the background.*

MINA: You are right about home, Lina. I've missed it too. I was just trying to get us through our journeys and keep us from remembering too much.

LINA: I know. I would have died without you. I was just trying to keep us from forgetting too much and becoming too empty like two hollow balloons floating aimlessly around the world.

BILLY: Mamas, you were so brave out there in the field of snow, I thought I would die of fright and lose my heart a second time.

GUATEMALAN MASSAGE THERAPIST: Here everybody we have to toast for the occasion. It's an old Guatemalan drink to celebrate escaping from impossible dangers unscathed.

TAXI DRIVER FROM UZBEKISTAN: And here, it's an old Uzbekistanian drink to celebrate victory over unleashed enemies and body thieves.

BILLY, TAXI DRIVER FROM UZBEKISTAN, GUATEMALAN MASSAGE THERAPIST: To Lina and Mina!

GUATEMALAN MASSAGE THERAPIST: To bodies in shape.

TAXI DRIVER FROM UZBEKISTAN: To hearts inside bodies in shape.

BILLY: To our new home.

TAXI DRIVER FROM UZBEKISTAN: Hey let's get out of here. They are starting to wake up.

Happy mellow music through the next section.

MINA: Our home will be sweet and small.

LINA: Our home will lack nothing at all.

BILLY: Our home will have a fruit market and a tiny mall.

MINA: Our home will be round as a ball.

GAUTEMALAN MASSAGE THERAPIST: With its many colors the whole world will enthrall.

LINA: We'll float boats in a tiny clear pond.

TAXI DRIVER FROM UZBEKISTAN: We'll bake bread that is crunchy and blonde.

GAUTEMALAN MASSAGE THERAPIST: We'll weave colored quilts from here and beyond.

LINA: We'll tell our story the worldwide.

MINA: We'll live in the desert, the city, the east side.

BILLY: And we'll always look on the bright side.

> *The music stops and the dreamy atmosphere is dissipated. The next lines are uttered in a matter of fact manner as if the characters had just returned from a long journey, tired but happy to be back home.*

MINA: Oh, it's good to be home.

LINA: Honey I'm home.

BILLY: Let's go home.

GAUTEMALAN MASSAGE THERAPIST: I wanna go home.

MINA: Honey, come home.

GAUTEMALAN MASSAGE THERAPIST: What a nice home.

TAXI DRIVER FROM UZBEKISTAN: I'm at home.

GUATEMALAN MASSGE THERAPIST: Home sweet home.

MINA: Make yourself at home.

LINA: There is no place like home.

BILLY: Home is where my heart is. That really brings it home.

home is so ingrained in our language, it's universal

MINA: Home is the place where, when you have to go there, they have to take you in.[1]

LINA: I want to stay home.

Very White Hitler Loving Woman and Irritated Immigration Officer get up from the massage tables in a trance, they put on Lina and Mina's space outfits and put the spaceship homes on their backs just as Lina and Mina used to do during their intergalactic travels and walk off stage. Blinding light.

THE END

---

[1] Verse from "The Death of the Hired Man" by Robert Frost.

The Town with Very Nice People. A Strident Immigrant Operetta

Runner up in the 2013 Jane Chambers Playwriting Contest

Jane Chambers Playwriting Award Jury evaluation noted: "the play's epic and festival storytelling, its explicit exploration of feminist themes, and the play's striking, distinctive main character. The wit, music, and cross-cultural perspective of this play invite experimental stagings."

"This mad, energetic work examines the metaphysics of the purely physical, and the casual cruelties of a life lived in a diaspora of culture, spirit and body. From its metempsychosis to its canny and comical portrayal of nasty, insular people both inside and outside of academia, this work is at once raw and funny, realistic and psychedelic, and beyond all, passionately human. Part Kafka, part Fornes, all Radulescu. It is rare that a playwright who is conscious of craft and particular of language writes a work that, with a complexity that vogues as simplicity, says exactly what she feels, and does not translate experience in primary, secondary, tertiary ways. In Radulescu's "strident operetta," this erudite writer places no poetic bulwark between the raw emotion and the words spoken; a Greek chorus of townspeople and academic bloviators annotate the anguish of a woman forced into emotional exile, who remains the most rooted and located of all characters in the work. Radulescu manages a deep compassion for even the grisliest of characters yet exposes with this work the struggles of women whose minds are too expansive for a belittling culture. Men's experience is considered universal, and the deepest of women's narratives is always deemed personal only to each individual woman. Radulescu's world teems with wide and collective life, a world that enchants and imprisons us all, and presents a radically feminist and deeply feminine portrait of a brilliant writer whose only true home is in her own refulgent spirit." **Endorsement by Deb Margolin, award winning playwright, recipient of 1999-2000 Obie award for Sustained Excellence in Performance.**

SETTINGS AND TIME FRAMES

The basic frame of the play is a tourist tour of a historic Small Southern Town. The tour itinerary intersects with the enigmatic life of the protagonist, Roxana Mincu. Some scenes take place in Small Southern Town, others in cities in the US or abroad. The chronology is non-linear and moves back and forth with flashbacks and flash forwards between the late nineties to the 2020s.

CHARACTERS (The director is encouraged to take liberties and assign several parts to each actor):

ROXANA – Romanian writer, artist, professor, and actress

ROXANA'S ALTER EGO – Only ROXANA and some choice characters can see ROXANA'S ALTER EGO

WOMAN FRIEND/LOVER OF ROXANA

LINDA – friend of ROXANA, college professor

DONNA – colleague of LINDA and ROXANA

MARK – lover of ROXANA

TOUR GUIDE – older local man doing the historic tours as a volunteer for the Visitor's Center in Town

CHORUS OF TOURISTS – young and old from different parts of the country, different professions and walks of life

CHORUS OF TOWNSPEOPLE – some are admirers others are enemies of ROXANA, all walks of life and ages

CHORUS OF UNIVERSITY MEMBERS – colleagues of ROXANA

MAX – son of ROXANA

RICK – son of ROXANA

A JUDGE

LAWYER 1 – attorney of ex-husband in ROXANA's divorce/custody trial

LAWYER 2 – ROXANA's attorney in divorce/custody trial

RE-ENACTERS

FRENCH RIVIERA ACTORS

MADONNA

Tableau I

The Historic Tour and Some Very Nice People

The Tour Guide is leading a group of tourists around the residential parts of Small Southern Town and on the tracks of famous people of Small Southern Town in the late 2000s. They get to an old white historic house in the Southern colonial style on a residential street in the center of town.

TOUR GUIDE: And this is the house where our Pulitzer Prize winner Roxana Mincu once lived. She wrote all her books in this house, including the one that won her the Pulitzer. People say she was a quiet neighbor except for a loud party she would throw once in a great while. She didn't like to be recognized in the street when she walked her dog and always wore a different pair of dark glasses and a hat, some form of disguise. And she didn't keep her front lawn very tidy, she liked it wild.

TOURIST CHORUS MEMBER 1: What happened to her? From all I know she is still alive.

TOUR GUIDE: She disappeared one day without a trace. Sold the house practically overnight and left without a word. Not even her closest neighbors and friends in town know of her whereabouts.

TOURIST CHORUS MEMBER 2: She had children, didn't she? Does anybody know what's become of them? They should know where their mother went. I hear she raised them by herself. I am writing a study on her life and work, a biography of sorts, and any lead to her life would help.

TOUR GUIDE: I think her kids moved to Europe, France or The Netherlands, I don't know, just rumors. Talking to some of her former colleagues who are still working or alive might help. And ... I don't know ...

Hesitates as if there is something he doesn't want to pursue.

TOURIST CHORUS MEMBER 2: What? Is there anything else you know about her? Please share!

TOUR GUIDE: Well, yes, you might find some important information at the courthouse, in the archives. She had a big trial in the nineties – a divorce and custody trial that was nasty – people from the town and the school got involved. They took sides and they dragged her personal life into the workplace. Apparently, it turned her off from this town forever, even though she continued living here and making a life here.

TOURIST CHORUS MEMBER 3: I don't blame her. I did hear that these courts here are horrendous, that they treat women terribly. And Blacks aren't very much liked either. And by the way what's with those confederate flags in front of some of the houses in town and on the hill up there just as you drive into town? Seriously? In this day and age? What are these people thinking? Or are they even thinking at all might be the better question.

TOUR GUIDE (*Slightly embarrassed and uneasy*): Well, it's the tradition, you know, a southern town with General Lee as our big hero ... It *is* part of our history. But the people here are real nice. Yea, there's some real nice people in this town.

TOURIST CHORUS MEMBER 1 (*Addressing Young Tourist Man*): Right, especially those who hang confederate flags on their doorsteps and those who persecute women in divorce trials.

TOUR GUIDE (*Taking on an offended tone*): Wait a minute, who said anything about persecution and women and Blacks being treated badly? I swear to God – you, liberal folk are always trying to find persecution at every step, you're just obsessed with persecution. What do you know about Roxana Mincu anyways?

TOWNSPEOPLE CHORUS MEMBER 1 (*Most likely both an insider and an outsider to Small Southern Town, having just joined the group out of mere curiosity*): I know that she was full of life and spark. That she always felt like an outsider in this town and she almost delighted in that outcast status.

TOURIST CHORUS MEMBER 1: It sounds like you are or were in love with her!

TOWNSPEOPLE CHORUS MEMBER 1 (*Dreamy, as if mulling over a pleasant memory*): Maybe I was. Many people were. Both men and women.

TOURIST CHORUS MEMBER 2: Excuse me, but what was your relationship with her? Are you from around here?

TOWNSPEOPLE CHORUS MEMBER 1: It's not important.

TOWNSPEOPLE CHORUS MEMBER 2: Are you talking about Roxana Mincu, the writer, so-called writer? She was a pill, that one, wasn't she!

TOWNSPEOPLE CHORUS MEMBER 3: She was vain and conceited. And she always dressed like she was going to a movie gala or something.

TOWNSPEOPLE CHORUS MEMBER 2: She said "fuck" in front of six-year-old children. She was obscene and something of a whore, if you ask me.

TOWNSPEOPLE CHORUS MEMBER 4: She was brilliant, passionate and witty.

TOWNSPEOPLE CHORUS MEMBER 3: She was not a Christian; she was more like the Devil if you ask me.

TOURIST CHORUS MEMBER 3: Nobody asked you, really. She sounds fascinating. I wonder where she might have gone. I wish I could meet her just once, even if briefly.

TOWNSPEOPLE CHORUS MEMBER 3: Oh, I met her plenty. I worked with her and got tired of her antics right fast. She was full of herself. And a strident bitchy voice she had – to put the frosting on the cake.

TOWNSPEOPLE CHORUS MEMBER 2: I heard she slept with half the town, men and women. She even slept with high school boys.

TOWNSPEOPLE CHORUS MEMBER 3: I heard she posed nude and she sat naked reading in her back yard.

TOWNSPEOPLE CHORUS MEMBER 2: And I don't think she was all that talented, if you ask me, just a lot of that female fluff with an ethnic touch. They love this feministic ethnic crap these liberals who give out them Pulitzers.

TOWNSPEOPLE CHORUS MEMBER 3: I bet you she slept with one of the people in the Pulitzer jury. I'm sure that's how she got the job at the university too. That's how these women get jobs these days. And immigrants too, stealing the jobs of honest Americans.

TOWNSPEOPLE CHORUS MEMBER 4: You people are disgusting, truly reprehensible. Has anybody seen her sleep with half the town, go out with high school boys, read naked in her back yard? And reading naked in one's backyard isn't illegal by the way; she had the right to do whatever she wanted on her property as long as she didn't hurt anybody. Her books are bestsellers all over the world, I guess she must have given blow jobs to a few million people to get them to buy and read her novels, hmm? No wonder she left here without even a good-bye, she was eaten alive, by conservatives and liberals alike, sexists and feminists. Some people just can't see a woman succeed and soar high. She didn't belong in this provincial confederate flag bigoted fucking little town, that's all.

TOURIST CHORUS MEMBER 1: Wow, I wish I would elicit so much talk and controversy when I die or disappear from my town. She certainly sounds interesting.

> *An old country song comes on, the light changes to a twilight mood and the tourists are dancing an old-fashioned dance like in a dream. The Tourist Chorus Members dance.*

(End of Tableau I)

Tableau II

The Good Lover

Inside Roxana's house in the mid-2000s. A balmy spring night filled with honeysuckle fragrances. Mark, Roxana's former lover has stopped by for a visit as he has passed through town. They are back together for a short while. The scene takes place in Roxana's bed and chronologically before the scene in the first Tableau.

ROXANA: I dreamed that my heart was the moon. Not "like" the moon, but *the* moon – round and fat and silly and shiny like the goddamn full moon. Why are we so obsessed with the moon? And my heart was freezing cold up there and I begged to get back to earth, back in my heart. Because my heart had left my body and had gone up there to be the fucking moon. And the place inside my body where my heart had been was a fucking big empty hole. And I was still alive. Such a disturbing dream!

MARK: I'm not surprised, you have a million lives, nothing kills you. I could never keep up with your imagination. I never know whether you are here in the moment or somewhere in one of your imaginary realms. I have always felt I was copy for your novels.

ROXANA: Oh, poor you! Such a neglected man you are, and on top of everything, also taken advantage of by insensitive female writer. Such a sad story, boo-hoo! How else can one live in this fucking provincial town without a demented imagination, tell me! How?

MARK: You seem to have managed well all these years – books, travels, beautiful house, piece of land with orchard, endowed professorship. Not bad for a refugee always complaining and bitching about something.

ROXANA (*She hits him jokingly with a pillow and then smacks him over the head gently*): Fuck you! What an asshole you are! It's easy for you to say that when you live in the big city, teach at a big research institution, have all the delights of an urban environment. That's why it could never work between us – you are such a fucking hypocrite, and an arrogant asshole.

MARK: You can be so sweet Roxana, I had forgotten how sweet and romantic you can be, particularly when something doesn't go your way and when you are mad. That's why *I* couldn't live with you!

ROXANA: And a good thing it is. We are both lucky to never have to live with one another. An occasional fuck whenever you pass through town on your way to DC is about as much as I can endure of your presence. At least you are a hot lover, not like some of the other assholes.

She laughs and stretches lazily, cuddling next to Mark.

MARK: Oh, thanks much Roxy, you always knew how to make a man feel good about himself. That's what I always loved about you.

ROXANA: I know, aren't I a sweet thing though? And yet you and I are so much alike, that's why it can never work between us. And you are the only one who gets me. A good thing it is we made a child together, it's the best thing two crazies like us could ever do with one another.

MARK: You're right, you and I could never get over each other and yet we are miserable together. That Max of ours is the distilled incarnation of all the happiness that could have existed between us but could never materialize – he is exactly that materializing.

ROXANA: Oh, how sweet, an actual moment of poetry from you. It's almost moving. Listen, I needed to talk to you seriously. There is something weird, something troubling and wicked going on in this town. I am more miserable than ever, you know. I've never fully adjusted here. Lately though I feel like I'm going crazy and that there are evil vibes floating around. Friends are becoming enemies, crazies with confederate flags are roaming around town like a bunch of unwashed psychos, people who have always greeted me in the past are now turning their heads when I pass them in the street and nobody invites me to any parties anymore. I never worried much about being accepted here or anything like that, but now it feels like there is downright hostility, conspiracy, I don't know – shit! I wish I could get the fuck out of here. Can't you get me a job at that university of yours? You know I'd be a superstar, right?

MARK: My love, you know I'd get you a job in a wink if I could. These ancient colleagues of mine refuse to either die or retire, what am I supposed to do, put arsenic in their coffee?

ROXANA: That's an excellent idea, why don't you try that? It would be your only real act of courage! No seriously, what do you think though about all this?

MARK: It sounds very much like more of the same thing you've always complained about. You just can't stand this fucking town! You couldn't stand it when you moved here fifteen years ago and you are never going to stand it any better, endowed professorship and orchard and garden full of beets and all. Nothing you tell me sounds new or something I haven't heard before.

ROXANA: Really? I think there is something new, a new element. Listen to this!

The setting changes to a party taking place right across the street from Roxana's house at Linda's house. Music, loud voices, laughter are being heard coming from the house.

(End of Tableau II)

Tableau III

The Feminist Party and Some Very Nice People

Inside Linda's House

LINDA: Hey everybody let's drink in honor of our friend Donna and celebrate her award. Beer anybody, wine, Champagne? Fill your glasses.

ROXANA'S ALTER EGO (*Enters the room and floats around the room teasing the guests*): Shouldn't I have been invited to this party Linda? Haven't I been a good friend, both your and Donna's friend? I thought you were all into inclusion, not exclusion, like a good feminist should be. Why have you shunned me Linda?

LINDA (*Who can only hear but not see Roxana's Alter Ego tries to mask her unease by whispering to her*): I didn't shun you Roxana, what the fuck! I invited whoever was on the list. It was Donna's list, Donna's award party. I didn't have to invite you if I didn't feel like it. Besides you're always so loud and so ... so ...

DONNA (*Surprised and unnerved by Linda's distraction*): Who the fuck are you talking to?

LINDA (*Trying to hide her unease and pretend nothing is wrong*): Sorry guys, I just got distracted for a second. I'm sort of emotional about Donna's award, it's a big day when true merit gets rewarded at our institution. She richly deserves it. To Donna! Congratulations.

ROXANA'S ALTER EGO (*Moving around Linda, teasing and tickling her*): Hey that was a bunch of phony nonsense. I am what? How am I exactly that you had to exclude me from this party? And to exclude me from other parties and events, you know what I'm talking about. Don't you think I have a heart? Has feminism eaten up your heart?

LINDA: I can invite whoever I want to my parties, just because you are my friend and neighbor doesn't mean I have to invite you to all my parties.

ROXANA'S ALTER EGO: Correct, only you should have invited me to *this* one and you know it. This one was different. And both as a friend and feminist you should have invited me. I will no longer call myself a feminist, I will call myself Femi-Freed.

> *Roxana's Alter Ego is heard giggling like crazy and repeating Freed, Freed... In the meantime, the women at the party start bad mouthing Roxana, but not really with invectives, in a subtler, more veiled manner while using feminist jargon.*

FEMALE GUEST: She isn't willing to destabilize the centrality of white middle class women.

LINDA: I know, right! She buys too much into a feminized image of womanhood, of herself. But she is great otherwise. I don't know, she's sort of ...

ROXANA'S ALTER EGO: Sort of what? Otherwise what? What the fuck, Linda, doesn't this sound phony to you, unimaginative and un-poetic? So, I like my lipstick and my sexy dresses, that's not where the essence of feminism lies. In any case, I will call myself Femi-Freed from now on. As if you were "freed" from something that shackled you before.

> *The women at the party indulge for a bit longer in criticizing and making fun of Roxana, her mannerisms, her accent, her dresses.*

FEMALE GUEST: You know when she sometimes speaks in faculty meetings, she is so off, sort of strident ...

LINDA: I know, right, she sometimes uses these convoluted sentences or words and makes jokes that nobody gets. She is great otherwise though, very smart. Only she can't possibly be on the advisory committee, she is not feminist enough, she is ... I don't know ... too foreign, too ...

> *Roxana's Alter Ego is heard giggling again and then sobbing deeply. She goes on floating around the room and whispering in the guests' ears.*

ROXANA'S ALTER EGO: Why didn't you include Biljana in this party and in the committee on the status of women? Why didn't you include me and Sonja and Sofia in the fucking committee? You talk so much about inclusion and hetero-centric this, and Eurocentric that, but you are all centric! You choose your own decentering and then make it centric and then start excluding other women that you don't like just like the good old boys always do. You create a different kind of provincialism, an ideological provincialism, a neo-liberal neo-feminist anti sassiness self-righteous ideological provincialism. Besides being morally wrong and hypocritical it's also so boring. Booooring! Where's the sass, where's the color, where's the spunk, where's the laughter and the humor? You lost it all talking too much about committees and hearing boards and leadership and cold jargon blah, blah, blah. Yet you break the hearts of your best friends and colleagues and exclude them and roll your eyes when you hear them talk and disagree with you in faculty meetings. I am starting the movement called Femi-Freedism – it's all about the freedom of mixing clashing colors, it's not about de fucking centering anyone but about creating lots of centers that all revolve around one another at some point – like some constellations – some stars move around a cluster and then that same cluster opens up and moves around the stars that had moved around them earlier. A constantly moving kaleidoscope. A never-ending dance of colors.

The guests at the party look dizzy, confused and embarrassed. They get more drinks and pair up or arrange themselves in small groups around the room and talk about the Dean and the administration of the university.

(End of Tableau III)

Tableau IV

The Reenactment and More Nice People

We are back in Small Southern Town, during the historic tour. More people have joined the tour, both tourists and locals who are intrigued by the animated conversations between the Tour Guide and the people in the group.

TOWNSPEOPLE CHORUS MEMBER 5: She had no friends. Except for a few weird women just like her with whom she would get together for some strange artsy-fartsy meetings.

TOWNSPEOPLE CHORUS MEMBER 6: Who are you talking about, may I know?

TOUR GUIDE: Stonewall Jackson. Here is the house of Stonewall Jackson. He taught at the Military Institute here and lived in this house for two years before he was called to serve the Confederacy. General Jackson ...

TOWNSPEOPLE CHORUS MEMBER 6: Were you talking about Stonewall Jackson? I thought it was a woman you were talking about.

TOURIST CHORUS MEMBER 4: Yes, we were talking about Roxana Mincu, the Pulitzer Prize winner. Do you know anything about her, what she was like, where she might have gone, what happened to her in the nineties in these courts here?

TOURIST CHORUS MEMBER 3: That's right, I am writing a study on her, a biography of sorts, and am trying to gather as much material about her as I can, since I know she lived here for over a quarter of a century and she was something of a figure in this town.

TOWNSPEOPLE CHORUS MEMBER 6: She sure was. And I heard this lady here say she had no friends except for "a few weird women like her." This couldn't be farther from the truth. She had lots of friends, men and women and the "weird women like her" who were among her best friends happened to be our best artists in the area, some with national and even international fame.

TOWNSPEOPLE CHORUS MEMBER 5: You mean like the photographer who made her children pose naked in her pictures? What an abomination, who can call that art?

TOWNSPEOPLE CHORUS MEMBER 1: Who can say it isn't? A discussion about what's art and what is not art is irrelevant anyways. We have a few artists of some renown in this town and instead of celebrating them you people put them down and invent all sorts of unseemly and primitive stories about them.

TOWNSPEOPLE CHORUS MEMBER 2: Why should we worry about the likes of Roxana Mincu and present this perverted image of our town to the tourists that visit it when we have people like Stonewall Jackson and General Lee to pride ourselves with?

TOUR GUIDE: Thank you, moving right along. General Jackson lived in this house with his third wife and ....

TOURIST CHORUS MEMBER 4: Funny, isn't it, that these generals are revered no matter how many wives and illegitimate children they had, while a woman's contributions to society and culture are all overlooked for petty gossip about her husbands and love affairs.

TOWNSPEOPLE CHORUS MEMBER 2: Oh, spare me the feminist rhetoric, will you. You people are going on and on about women's rights this and women's rights that, as if all there is to women's rights is the right to be promiscuous.

TOWNSPEOPLE CHORUS MEMBER 1: It's one of them. If men can, why can't women be promiscuous? Equality is equality. Look, we live in a little provincial town in the middle of nowhere. Tourists come and go through here every single day of the year going to the Stonewall Jackson House, the goddamn Horse of General Lee – Traveler, and the Lee Chapel. There is no critical view of these figures who supported the confederacy and slavery. You can no longer pretend this is ok in our age when racism is rampant all over again, as if we never had a civil rights movement. But things evolve and change, and so does this town. We also have other people who have achieved renown beyond the frontiers of the town, and we should celebrate them too, whether we agree with their lifestyles or not. I agree with the tourist here, that the confederate flags hanging in front of some houses are sort of shameful. Not to mention that we've been visited lately by the very Klan, who left sinister fliers on people's doorsteps and on campus. We should all stand up to such bigotry, particularly after what happened in the neighboring city last year...

> *At that point a parade of re-enactment of confederate soldiers is marching by and singing Dixie while waving around large confederate flags. People from the county are also in the parade; the parade has a ghostly feel to it. Lighting should be gloomier and the atmosphere eerie. The people in the historic tour stare at the parade in disbelief.*

TOURIST CHORUS MEMBER 3: Man, don't these people ever wash? It seems to me that more than anything else, they are at war with water and soap. How could such displays be allowed in public these days? What kind of town is this anyways?

> *People in the group laugh heartily while the tourist guide looks distressed.*

TOURIST GUIDE: That is such a stereotype you people. I'm done with this group. I've never seen a more disrespectful group of tourists in my life.

Roxana's Alter Ego appears in a red gauzy dress swirling and dancing around the tourist guide and teasing him. He thinks he is losing his mind and starts waving his hands at the apparition in a chaotic agitated manner. In this scene only the person next to whom Roxana's Alter Ego is standing can see her while all others cannot.

ROXANA'S ALTER EGO: Oh Mr. TOURIST GUIDE, don't be upset! Aren't you tired of doing the same damn tour every single fucking day of the year for twenty years and saying the same damn lies over and over again, about General Lee and General Jackson? How about the new town, how about the women, the Blacks, the side streets and the hidden areas, the houses of the artists, the weird artists, the gay artists, the industrial artists? There is more to this town than General Lee's fucking stuffed horse.

The Guide acts as if possessed by spirits, writhing and moaning and waving his hands, to the great delight of the tourists. Then Roxana's Alter Ego moves to the Townspeople Chorus Member 1 and embraces him in a warm embrace.

ROXANA'S ALTER EGO: Thanks Rick, you've always been a good friend. You were the only one who stood by me in the nineties too. The trial, the university politics, the people whispering and exchanging looks when I passed by – how boring and how primitive and how it tore me apart. But you've always been the cool guy. We could have been lovers you know ... I always thought you were sort of a hunk.

She is swirling around him laughing.

TOWNSPEOPLE CHORUS MEMBER 1: Now, you're telling me! I've been crazy about you all these years. If only I had known, I would have been bolder you know ... I would have ...

ROXANA'S ALTER EGO: I had to keep true to my promise-never fuck anyone local. And I didn't. It's fascinating to hear what all these people have invented about me – it appears I screwed the entire local population of high school boys among other things too – what a bunch of phonies!

> *She disappears in the same swirling dizzying motions and haze that she appeared in, leaving everybody in the two groups slightly dizzy and confused. For just a few short moments the people in the tour group all gather in an opera kind of stylized tableau with their arms stretched out while a group of the Townspeople who were against Roxana make a similar operatic group to counteract the first. The scene should be stylized and over the top, surreal.*

TOURIST CHORUS MEMBERS (*In a rhythmic singing mock-opera tone addressing Roxana's Alter Ego, speaking to the thin air*): Don't go Roxana, don't go, don't go, don't go! Tell us your story, tell us the truth, tell us where you are! Don't go Roxana, don't go, please don't go!

TOWNSPEOPLE CHORUS MEMBERS (*Responding in a war like fashion to the first group*): Go away, go away, go away! Never come back, you bring bad luck and the Devil's curse, you bring bad luck, go away and never come back.

TOURIST CHORUS MEMBERS: You people are bad, you are sad, you are mad, don't let Roxana go, she is so, so ... oh no! You don't want to have a town of lame confederates thriving and going so low. Stay Roxana, don't go, please, don't go, you are our only hope of a hip town that doesn't blow.

The scene ends with the group of the Confederate re-enactment passing through in exaggerated warrior and battle poses, then singing Dixie with exaggerated fervor and patriotism while the Tourist Chorus performs a modern exaggerated number on hip hop music.

(End of Tableau IV)

Tableau V

The Trial, a Lot of Nice People and the Screws Business

The scene takes place inside the local courthouse of Small Southern Town. Roxana is wearing a black and white suit, her hair is pulled back and she is at the stand, during her own divorce trial. The Judge is a morose older man who mumbles his words into his beard. There are also colleagues from Roxana's workplace.

LAWYER 1: Ms. Mincu, have you or not committed adultery and ...

LAWYER 2: Objection Your Honor, irrelevant for custody!

JUDGE: Overruled, relevant for mother's moral influence on the child. Answer or I'll hold you in contempt.

ROXANA: I am in a relationship other than with my soon to be ex-husband right now.

LAWYER 1: That is still adultery as you are not yet legally divorced. Did you have intercourse with another man while still living with your husband?

LAWYER 2: Your Honor, where is this leading, we are discussing custody of Ms. Mincu's and Mr. Brian's son Rick, Ms. Mincu's abilities as a parent, this is not relevant to custody ...

JUDGE: It's all relevant. The parents' moral values are relevant to the upbringing of the child. Answer the question Ms. Mincu. In the Virginia Commonwealth adultery is a class 4 misdemeanor. As are sodomy and buggery, didn't you know that Mr. Lawyer 2?

ROXANA: ...

Silence. She is looking straight at the Judge without answering.

JUDGE (*Getting angrier*): Answer the question or I'll hold you in contempt of court. And for your information Mr. Lawyer 2, it *is* relevant for custody. See Brown v. Brown, 218 Va. 196 (1977).

ROXANA (*Makes a sign to her Lawyer to approach her. Lawyer 2 approaches her and she whispers to him.*): Can't I take the fifth?

LAWYER 2 (*Whispering back to Roxana.*): I'll try but the Judge can find a waiver. (*Speaking louder towards the Judge.*) Your Honor my client refuses to answer the question and asserts her privilege pursuant to the Fifth Amendment of the U.S. Constitution, and of Article 1, section 8 of the State Constitution.

JUDGE (*Staring into space for a while*): All right! You'll get your Fifth for now, but we'll get Ms. Mincu another way. If it's not buggery or adultery, then we'll get her for stealing. Send in the next witness.

Next witness is a colleague of Roxana's from her university. Skinny mustached man from a different department comes in looking angry and is directed to sit at another witness stand in the room.

LAWYER 1: Can you tell us if you recognize this person sitting there on that stand?

UNIVERSITY CHORUS MEMBER: Of course, I can, it's ROXANA Mincu, she teaches some kind of creative writing and has the biggest mouth on campus.

LAWYER 2: Objection your Honor, unnecessary slandering.

LAWYER 1: Tell us what happened recently between yourself and Ms. Mincu and the reason for your complaint about her to the Dean of the University.

UNIVERSITY CHORUS MEMBER: Ms. Mincu simply stole my children's crib.

LAWYER 1: Can you be more explicit, please, how exactly did she do that?

UNIVERSITY CHORUS MEMBER: My wife and I had lent her the crib that that we had used for our children, for her own new born child and when we asked her to return it to us just recently, once she was done using it for her son, there were parts missing from the crib.

LAWYER 1: What parts exactly were missing?

UNIVERSITY CHORUS MEMBER: Two screws were missing from the crib and it could never be put together again.

LAWYER 1: So basically Ms. Mincu destroyed the crib in which your children had slept during their infancy and then she stole two screws which made it impossible for the crib to be reassembled and used ever again.

LAWYER 2: Your Honor, objection, this is ridiculous and misleading. She didn't steal anything; she returned all the parts of the crib and had misplaced two screws. Are we going to bicker over two screws in the middle of a divorce and custody trial of this magnitude?

JUDGE: It is up to me Mr. Lawyer 2 to decide what we are to bicker about or not. All this is relevant for the character of the mother: adulteress, buggerer and thief.

LAWYER 2: The said crib was a family heirloom that Mr. Colleague had entrusted Ms. Mincu with, and she deceived his trust and destroyed a valuable possession. And then refused to pay the damages and Mr. Colleague was then forced to appeal to the Dean of the University to be recompensed for the damage done to the crib. Ms. Mincu, were you not aware that you had destroyed Mr. Colleague's heirloom crib?

ROXANA: It was a Kmart crib already in bad shape when he gave it to me, and he asked me to pay $250 in damages for the crib. A brand new one at Kmart costs only $150. He took me to the office of the Dean and complained about an honor violation and made me pay $250 for a crib that wasn't worth that much even new.

JUDGE: Quiet in court! I will hold you I contempt Ms. Mincu. Speak only when you are asked a question.

ROXANA: I was just asked a question your Honor!

JUDGE(*Gets all red and screams at the top of his lungs*): Sileeeeeeeeence in cooooooooourt!

> *A group of colleagues from the university and townspeople come into the courtroom in a chorus like formation and perform an exaggerated melodramatic number about the screws in the Colleague's crib.*

Combined CHORUSES OF UNIVERSITY AND TOWNSPEOPLE:

ROXANA you're a thief, thief, thief,

You stole nails from a crib, crib, crib

Tomorrow you'll steal a whole crib and a gold leaf

After tomorrow you'll hammer a nail into the rib

Of an innocent victim or even our Lord Jesus Christ

You're an adulteress and a whore

You wear red and you always want more

You are the shame of our town

You will be punished, punished bad

And you'll wear a big ugly crown

Made of thorns and of worms and of crib nails

To teach you a lesson and make you sad

And make you wail

And make you look pale

And make you dead like a crib nail.

> *The musical number must reach a high level of grotesqueness and make the audience feel embarrassed. It has to progress almost sexually towards an orgasmic moment. Then the group moves threateningly towards Roxana and tries to swallow her, but after a few moments in which it appears like she has been suffocated and swallowed up by the group in a voracious manner, she emerges out of it victoriously looking like the image of Liberty in the painting of Delacroix, with one breast uncovered and stepping over bodies.*

ROXANA (*Singing in Grandiose Opera Style*):

You will not destroy me oh no,

You will not eat and swallow me oh no,

You are evil destructive and confederate people so go

Your niceness, your fake smiles and your hellos

You can stick them up there where the sunshine don't go

So, go, so go, so go!

I will find justice and tell my story high and low

Or maybe on second thought I will burn down the town

Like I saw in a movie called *Dogville* so cool

Where the heroine was raped and mocked and hurt

By nice people like you in this town of dirt

And at the end of the movie she burns down the town

And erases it from the face of the earth

And goes on living her life full of mirth!

> *Roxana becomes wild and fierce like a Fury. Her two children appear like angels gliding graciously into the court room and try to calm her down.*

RICK AND MAX (*Singing and Performing a Cheerful Number*):

Oh, mama, oh mama don't burn down the town

We live here too and it's best to calm down

These are just ignorant republican clowns

They're not worthy of your ire and fires

They are just a bunch of small-town liars

Better let's plant a garden, write a poem, or make a show

Better write to the newspaper for other people to know

Your story, our story of discrimination and alienation

Your story our story of sadness and frustration

And from the garden, the show, the poem will grow

A new little town of cheer and glow

Of kindness and fun

But for now, can we please just run!

> *The Children and Roxana all glide out of the courtroom in a swoop. They could be attached to strings so they can be lifted up and so it looks as if they are flying out of the room despite everybody else's attempts to hold them down and catch them.*

(End of Tableau V)

Tableau VI – Play Ending Number One

Roxana's Paradise

Roxana is talking amorously with her lover Mark at a table in a café on the French Riviera.

ROXANA: Well we did it! Finally, I had the courage to break away and free myself from all that ballast – the small-town academic job with good benefits and big house with lots of land and lots of polluting weight. I feel like a bird in the sky, like a fish gliding through salty waves and all the metaphors. I never thought you'd have the ovaries to do it. Doesn't it feel good, don't you feel free?

MARK (*Smiling ironically and flirtatiously*): I'll never be free if I'm in love with you Roxana. You keep me in your spell.

ROXANA: Oh pleeeaase, spare me the cheap clichés and romantic tropes. No, seriously, doesn't it feel great, freeing? I must say I feel deliciously vindicated. To have seen my department chair's face when I told him I was resigning, a week before classes started!!! And then the Dean's face – it was all worth it – to have that satisfaction of a fantasy come true. The only thing that bugs me is: why didn't I do it earlier? Why did I wait so long to break away and to shake off the chains of that job and of that town that made me so miserable for so long? Have any idea Mark?

MARK (*Laughing wholeheartedly*): Wow, you are asking me for my opinion? This will have been a good day. Before you know it, you'll be asking me for advice and the world as we know it will end. You weren't ready to take this step earlier and you did it when you felt ready. And it wasn't all as bad as you make it sound. You raised your boys there, they liked growing up in the beautiful mountains, they had happy childhoods, didn't they? And you enjoyed some parts of your sojourn in the little historic town in the middle of the Blue Mountains. You wrote some of your best books there. What am I talking about – you wrote your very best work there.

ROXANA: Out of suffering and boredom and hatred! Great sources of inspiration!

MARK: That's how most great works are created – out of exactly those three things you mentioned: suffering, boredom and hatred. Wow – you got all three of them all at the same time. You always take it all, don't you!

ROXANA (*Slapping him jokingly over his back*): Fuck you Mark! And also, not fuck you! I don't know maybe you are right. But then also I am really sick of this creative paradigm of having to suffer and be on the verge of suicide and torn into a million pieces in order to create something worthwhile that still ends up rotting on some back shelf of some forgotten bookstore – if you're lucky and it hasn't been all remaindered – you know like shredded to a whole bunch of paper shreds.

MARK: Yes, I know what to be remaindered means, several of my books met that fate. It's how it always is -- the best art comes from suffering.

ROXANA: Fucking bullshit clichés! How about from joy and pleasure and laughter! I couldn't have written any of what I have written, had I not experienced all of that.

MARK: That's true, but neither could you have written anything you have written without being torn apart into so many pieces as you always say, without all your anguishes, sufferings, the obstacles you had to overcome.

ROXANA: Oh crap! You sound like a fucking academic. Or a preacher! I'm sick of the torn apart and the sufferings and obstacles. How about just plain bubbling colorful fluffy sensuous happiness for a while? I am shifting my worldview and inspiration. I am breaking this paradigm of the suffering artist because it's fucking bullshit. How about the laughing, joyful artist?

MARK: Ok, go for it my love. I may sound like a fucking academic, but you sound like a fucking Hallmark card.

ROXANA: Hey Dante's *Paradiso,* you know the last book of the *Divina Commedia* is all about beauty and happiness and beatitude and floating around in the blue heavens with God at your side and some cute angels flying around. I want to capture that. I want to create something of that nature only for modern readers.

MARK: Go ahead my dearest, you have my support like you always did. Puzzle, dazzle, bedazzle me with your modern *Paradiso.*

> *Men and women from the nearby beaches and streets of this luminous French Riviera town move in jazzy dance steps and perform another operetta number. They circle Roxana and perform the number with her and for her. The cast of this number is racially and ethnically diverse. The chorus line they sing is as follows:*

FRENCH RIVIERA ACTORS: You think the world is bad and hopeless?

Violence, rape, war, genocide and stress?

Too much technology, torture and alienation?

Global warming, pandemics and overpopulation?

Cheer up, relax, swim with us in the deep blue sea

Your fretting and agony won't change a thing, you see!

Better follow the advice of our darling Voltaire

"Cultivate your garden" and don't despair!

Enjoy the sand, the water, the food, the diversity

Forget your anger, your past, forget your university!

Roxana, oh Roxana, you are the bomb

You inspire us and to your charms we succumb!

Enjoy life, write happy plays such as this light operetta

Don't you wanna spread happiness, you'd better!

Don't you wanna spread joy, laughter and cheer!

Don't you wanna swirl with us here on this magical sphere!

This beautiful planet, or better even, have a beer!

> *Roxana is being swirled around in the wild dance and falls on the dancer's arms at the end of the number like a Broadway star, jubilant and radiant. Mark applauds, then gets up, goes towards Roxana and takes her hand inviting her to dance. The music changes to a slow dance and they dance languorously as the lights are getting dimmer in a blue, dreamy hue.*

(End of Tableau VI)

Tableau VII

Play Ending Number Two

The Accident

Roxana is alone on a park bench in an American city. She is talking on her cell phone and calling friends and family. She has a small suitcase next to her.

ROXANA: I don't know Mark, I just resigned from my university job, sold my house and drove here to this goddamn American city where I feel just as lost and lonely, with the only difference that nobody recognizes me and smiles their dumb smiles at every street corner. Why can't you meet me here and we can go away together? I can write all the books I have in mind and you can write about all the books you have in mind and maybe you and I will get it together before we die. The world is so fucked up already, our lives are so fucked up, maybe we can start over or something cliché like that.

Roxana is listening for a while and repeating some of Mark's words, oscillating between anger and excitement.

ROXANA: Yes, I did sort of do all that overnight: resign, sell my house, and get on the road. It's just as I had always imagined it. It felt good. Up to now everything is as planned, except for you here next to me ...

Pause in which we deduce that Mark interrupts her.

ROXANA: I don't know what got into me to suddenly be nice and sweet, maybe my new freedom and maybe the fact that this new freedom comes with a maddening degree of loneliness. What the fuck am I supposed to do here on this motherfucking bench in this big American city all by myself without a job, without a friend, with my kids spread all over the world, my parents both dead, with no country, no home? Back to where I started thirty years ago? Only I am thirty fucking years older. ....

Pause in which Mark interrupts her again.

ROXANA: No, I'm not trying to be melodramatic, you know it's not my style. I could always go back to my mother land – Ha! Wouldn't that be the ultimate defeat, and wouldn't I be the laughingstock of the press and the journalists and my beloved family who reneged me. I see the headlines already: "American writer of Romanian origins returns to her native country!" or even better: "Pulitzer Prize winner of Romanian origins returns to her mother land after career stall in America!"

Mark's voice is heard talking angrily on the other line.

ROXANA: You what? Say, you what? You got married? You fucking got married? ... Of course, I'm swearing, what the fuck do you want me to do? Allow me to be a bit surprised, to hear the man who vowed eternal love to me, who vowed to never marry again, who vowed he would always jump to my rescue whenever I needed him, who vowed he would always be honest and upfront with me, to have this same man announce to me that he got married. I thought that was the kind of relationship you wanted, free, wild, unpredictable, brutally honest. I thought we were soul mates forever no matter how badly we got along. Alright fuck you and your dumb bride!

> *Roxana hangs up and stares into space for a while. She gets up and starts crossing the street on the red light carrying her luggage. Her suitcase gets stuck on the pavement and a car going full speed runs her over. A long silence follows with no sounds of any kind. Roxana is lying in the middle of the street with her suitcase open and things from it strewn all over the street.*

ROXANA (*She gets up, shakes the dust and dirt off her clothes and stuffs the pile of clothes and underwear inside the suitcase*): Shit! This isn't how it's supposed to end. What the fuck! I will not accept this kind of ending to my life ... play ... whatever...

> *She plays the crossing of the street and the car running her over backwards as if in rewind and we see her again sitting on the same bench talking on her cell phone.*

ROXANA: Yes sweetheart, I have done all that, we only live once. It feels great, I feel like a new person. A whole new beginning at fifty. I'll wait for you here on this bench, the little park at the corner of Randolph and Maine. Yes, you know I've always liked corners and crossroads. See you soon darling.

> *Roxana waits a while, checks her phone, applies lipstick, lights a cigarette. A red-haired good-looking woman in her fifties comes along. Roxana jumps up happily from the bench and the two women embrace and kiss passionately.*

ROXANA: Finally, at last! We did it! Where should we go? There's a whole wide world out there!

WOMAN LOVER of ROXANA: Honey I'll go to the end of the world with you. But for now, let's just have lunch.

> *Roxana picks up her suitcase and takes the woman's arm. They both walk off happily.*

ROXANA (*She winks at the audience*): Now that's a good ending, isn't it!

(End of Tableau VII)

Tableau VIII

Play Ending Number Three

The Funeral

Roxana is lying dead in a coffin in a room filled with huge wreaths of flowers of all colors. Family, friends, and colleagues are all gathered in silence around her coffin talking about her life and her character.

MAX (*Roxana's youngest son, speaks in a loud whisper*): Mama would have hated all this: the quiet, the huge wreaths, the whispering, and the pretense grief. She would have loved a big rowdy party with loud music and dancing and drinking for her funeral. She often said she wanted to die and be buried the way she lived: wildly, passionately, recklessly. Big! She lived big and she would have loved a big party. Whose idea was it anyways to have this masquerade of a funeral? Look at this: some of her worst enemies from the university are here pretending they care, just to look good and feel good about themselves. I know what she would have to say about them.

RICK (*Roxana's oldest son, answering in the same loud whisper*): She would say something like this: "look at the phony motherfuckers, they treated me like shit while I was alive and now they are all grief and tears at my death. Screw them!"

Max and Rick laugh out loud, drawing severe looks from the rest of the people gathered at the funeral.

MAX: That's exactly what she would say, you got it bro! I miss her so much. We'll never have another mama like our mama! She took no prisoners and lived every minute like it was her last. Say, how about we throw out all these stogy bastards and have the kind of party that mama would have liked, hmm?

Max and Rick throw everybody out of the room at the great indignation and outrage of the university folk who were Roxana's colleagues. Only the handful of her best friends stay, mostly women from the town and from other parts of the country and the one man with a crush on Roxana from the town.

RICK: Hey Folks, let us throw a real party the way Roxana, our mother would have liked it, let us celebrate her life and remember her the way she would have liked it.

WOMAN FRIEND OF ROXANA 1: She always made me laugh on every occasion.

WOMAN FRIEND OF ROXANA 2: She made me see things and the world in a new light, always attentive to details that no one else seemed to notice.

MIDDLE-AGED MAN WHO LOVED ROXANA (*He is the same as Townspeople Chorus Member 1*): There was no one around here with her spirit and her sex appeal. With her style! If only I had made love to her once...

WOMAN FRIEND OF ROXANA 1: She had the courage to say what nobody else did, she stood up for what she believed was right even when everybody else shunned her for it ... It drove some people crazy!

Roxana gets up from her coffin and starts talking. Everybody is utterly shocked and spooked.

ROXANA: I saw this trick in a Woody Allen movie and also in a play by a French playwright– the dead person getting up from their coffin and talking at their own funeral. You learn stuff from movies and plays that can save your life. Everything is possible in a play. This is not a good ending though. In fact, it sucks – too melodramatic, too weepy, too sweet. Though I really appreciate what you all had to say about me. I guess one needs to die to really know who one's true friends really are. I think I'll stick around for a while longer. Let's just have a big party to celebrate my resurrection.

> *Rock music starts playing and everybody dances with abandon.*

(End of Tableau VIII)

Tableau IX

The Class. Last Ending

A university class somewhere on the east coast. Mark, Roxana's former lover is discussing her works to a Contemporary American Literature class.

MARK: So, as I was saying Roxana Mincu's works illustrate a certain kind of feminist post-modern aesthetics of rupture, of liminality and disjointed realms in a continuous search for the real, for the real ...

> *Roxana walks in wearing a flowery red dress, humming Bruce Springsteen's song "I'm on fire." Then she sits down in one of the classroom chairs pretending to listen to Mark. The students are all in awe. Mark is both angry and hugely embarrassed.*

ROXANA: Aesthetics of rupture my ass! What do you know about my liminality and disjointed realms, Mark? You are now an expert in my "feminist" works? And you are supposed to be this great feminist? Remember when I called you from a park bench in the big city after I left the provincial southern town and sold everything, and I needed you and you told me you had gotten married? That was quite a noble feminist act, I dare say.

MARK: Roxana, I thought you were dead. I thought you were run over by a car. Did you survive the accident?

ROXANA: Yes, I survived the fucking accident. I turned it all back. I'm a writer, remember, I can change my own ending. A bit disappointed, hmm?

> *The students are all looking in awe at Roxana and applauding after each one of her lines, as if she were a character in a play.*

MARK: Not a bit disappointed Roxana, more like relieved. Now I don't have to have you on my conscience forever. I knew that ending was a bit too tragic, not tragic enough, too melodramatic: a deux ex-machina kind of ending. Not your style. And by the way, I divorced my wife. You were right, as always, I was never made for marriage and it got to be so dull after a while, the whole marriage thing. You spoiled me, what can I say, everything seems dull after you Roxana.

ROXANA: I've tried several endings myself and none of them seemed to work. There is no perfect ending, they are all just lame attempts to put a knot in this ridiculous thread of our lives. Still, there's got to be a better ending out there, an ending like a crushed rainbow with colors bleeding all over the canon of Western literature. An ending that doesn't conclude anything but that leaves everything suspended beautifully in the process of existence like a group of ballet dancers frozen in their most gracious acrobatic stunning pose.

MARK: If there has ever been anyone capable of creating such an ending, that would be you Roxana. And that is only because you have blurred all distinctions between your life and your art, that's it. I get it now, if there was a prize for how artfully one lives one's life, you would get it.

ROXANA: Are you making fun of me? My life is so artfully lived that I would get a fucking prize for it in the universe of people prizing how one lives one's life? Really? What the fuck are you talking about? You are confusing all these students here. My life has been one huge mess after another, heartbreaks and failures and ruptures and breakups and unfulfilled yearnings. That would get me a fucking prize?

MARK: Yes Roxana, the way you have trimmed and framed all that with a stylish entrance or an eccentric exit, a flamboyant dress swirling amid rubble and heartache, a soulful hand touch in the midst of chaos. The way you've tied lose ends, connected events, anticipated tragedies, wove it all in colorful quilts and circles. That would get you a prize.

The students in the class are applauding enthusiastically and admiringly.

ROXANA: I don't want a fucking prize. I don't want eternal life. All I want is a good ending. What makes us original? It's not in the actual ingredients, it's in the combination of the ingredients and the timing. A perfect ending would be for me to return to the Town with Very Nice People on a white horse riding along Main Street through the very center of the town and rescue my Alter Ego, my soul mate, my ghost as she is whining and grieving there since my departure. I would pick her up with one swoop of my right arm and like in the movies place her on the horse and we would ride madly through town and out of the town in a swirl of dust and gallop into the twilight and out of everybody's sight. That would be a good ending.

A student in the class is desperately raising her hand. Mark asks her to say what she wants to say.

STUDENT: Professor, will all this be on the exam?

All other students are aghast at the question and roll their eyes.

ROXANA: See, that's why Eugene Ionesco has his teacher character stab his student character to death at the end of his play *The Lesson.*

(End of Tableau IX)

Tableaux X

The Town of Multicolor. Final, Final Ending for Real

We are back in Small Southern Town and the historic tour of the town in 2025. The tourists and the Tour Guide and all the passers-by who have gathered along the way are back on Main Street ending their tour. Roxana appears on a white horse all dressed in white, looking majestic like an apparition from a fairy tale or an old movie. She rides through the center of town in the middle of Main Street and faces the group of tourists.

ROXANA: Well hello everybody, all you "very nice people" and good old Southern Town. I've travelled the world looking for answers about what is wrong with this town and the university in it and I was also looking for towns and universities that are worse, more bigoted, more Confederate, more stifling than this one, thinking I wouldn't find a worse one, but I did. Only in America!

Roxana starts humming a soulful old Gypsy melody beckoning her ghost, double, Alter Ego who has been waiting for her. The two embrace for a long time as if melting into one another.

ROXANA: From now on this will be the town of simulacra and created realities. In each corner of the town, there will be enactments of real and imagined events, of historical events and of personal stories. This is the beginning and the end of the Historic Tour of the Town. And here is our guest keynote speaker, no other than Madonna.

MADONNA (*She appears from around one of the corners and dances her way to meet Roxana*): Hey people and you Roxana! Thanks for making me part of this play, right? I think you need yet another ending, past the ending, the utopian ending. This here will be the corner of beauty, unexpected joys and the professions – a corner where painters and writers, bakers and welders make things touched by Multicolor. I'd love to help you all and particularly you Roxana. I went on tour to your country and your people were crazy about me though they didn't take it very well when I told them that they should stop treating Gypsies like shit. They're a racist bunch, too, you know. But in any case, you find racists everywhere, right? The important thing is to try to make things better. That's why I came here to the boonies to help you turn this fucking town around and make it the town of Multicolor.

ROXANA and MADONNA (*The two women rap together this section with the town cheering and accompanying the rapping*): We'll have poems and iron figurines, portraits and gluten free bread, stories and croissants, landscapes of sunrise with iron birds, a corner of the making and of the creating, of watching and nourishing, of hard and soft things. We'll have objects that feel glossy to the touch and that enrapture you with their explosion of Multicolor, music made of leaves and crystal beads that shine and break the light in a thousand nuances of crimson and Amarillo.

WOMAN LOVER OF ROXANA: Right over here in this other corner, women of Multicolor and women of the movement of Femi-Freedism give birth to ideas that are like real flesh and blood creatures. They also give birth to brown clay babies. Oh, them brown clay babies you want to eat them up. And you can. The babies made of brown clay have magical powers, they are the anti-magical magic babies that look pretty and are well crafted from brown and red clay taken from the surrounding gardens and hills in the area, all waiting for someone to breathe life into them. Sister Madonna here gives birth to brown clay babies and then places them in stacks inside the travel agency. The women of Multicolor take the brown clay babies birthed by Madonna and breathe life into them, breathe the life of ideas into them. This here will be the utopia of the new world. In this new world, you can eat words when you are hungry and drink words when you are thirsty.

> *Clowns and acrobats fill the street and all the street corners with colorful movements and hula hoops. An operatic grand finale ensues where all the different corners perform and sing in coordination and harmony with each other, while also contrasting each other. The following lines are supposed to be performed in a dynamic rhythm with music and choreography like in a grandiose musical finale or an opera finale.*

MADONNA (*While she is giving birth to Brown Clay Babies*): Just like a virgin, I am birthing delicious brown clay babies that sing in all the languages. Anyone wants a multilingual brown clay baby? They will make the world a better place, oh yea. I am sexy and I know it, and like a virgin I give birth to delicious brown clay babies that will teach you foreign languages, they are the Rosetta babies, you eat one of these babies and you will immediately start speaking Finish and Urdu, Portuguese and Japanese, Mongolian and Latin.

MARK (*Who has suddenly appeared on a witch's broom*): Shit, this fucking broom is hard to ride for someone with a penis between their legs. I suppose that's why most witches are women, they are better at riding the damned brooms, because they have vaginas. I know this sounds sort of sexist, but what the fuck, it's easier to ride a broom when you have a vagina than a penis, it's a fact. (*He is saying the previous lines softly, as an aparté, making sure Roxana doesn't hear it, and then starts talking louder again.*) Roxana, you are seeing your dream come true, Dante's *Divina Commedia* in post-modern shape. You have created the perfect town and written the perfect ending. Good and bad, corny and horny, edgy and silly, gross and exquisite, terrifying and yellow, all here in one small Southern Town and all here in one play ending.

You'll be written up in history books and in performance theory studies. Feminists and anti-feminists both will claim you, post-modernists and classicists both will defend you, and I for one, have only one question: Will you marry me Roxana? I rode all the way here to Small Southern Town on a witch's broom to ask you if you will marry me?

ROXANA: You mean marry you in that un-marrying un-Hollywood, un-romantic way? Marry you like create peace, order and disorder and negotiate the chaos of our lives under the rule of Multicolor together? You and me? And how about Woman Lover? I can't leave her out, I love her just as much, I can't live without her. And how about Alter-Ego? Do you want to un-marry marry me in a ménage à four? Save the world, open a Brown Babies Who Turn into Cool Ideas Factory, buy the Community Bank and turn it into a magical skating ring for recent war refugees from Syria and Iran and Rwanda and Honduras and Transylvania? Open a non-allergenic bread factory and feed the world? Make Rosetta babies and speak all the languages?

MARK: That's exactly what I was thinking Roxana, but you said it better than I could have ever said it. I promise I'll develop new and more inventive pedagogies to teach your life and work you deserve the best pedagogies in the world ... Roxana, I've changed, you've changed me. I've become a welder instead of an academic. I am a welder of souls and fire birds. Our house will quiver with exquisitely welded products, rainbow glass products and multicultural children.

> *Roxana's children Rick and Max appear riding white horses into town. They reach the corner of random moments of beauty and sadness about the human condition.*

MAX: Mama, it's good to be home. Finally, we have our dream town. I had missed it so badly all these years, traveling around the world.

RICK: We told you Mama, long time ago during your bad, bad trial to not burn down the town. I agree with Max, it's good to be home. Home. You did it, Mama. Max and I will open a drugstore for the melancholy and the irate. We'll play rock and roll, punk rock, Bach and Chopin all day in unpredictable order. We'll build two magic boxes: one for horrendous memories that people want to get rid of but still want to have a record of, and one for exquisite and soothing memories that people might have lost or forgotten but need to get to in order to get over their horrendous memories. We'll keep the memory of the town; nothing will be lost.

ROXANA: I knew my boys will save the day. I've missed you terribly. Where have you sons been all this time?

RICK: We've been everywhere around the world, just like you taught us mama, we even attended your goddamn funeral, remember? We visited everybody else's homeland and learned Somalian recipes and Norwegian dances, Senegalese deserts and Latvian acrobatics.

MAX: But then one day Rick pointed to me a dogwood tree in bloom somewhere in a remote village at the other end of the earth at the same altitude as our small southern town and its delicate flowers got to me and reminded me of the dogwood tree in our front yard in which Max and I used to always climb and make a tree house when we were kids. We keeled over with yearning for the town of our childhood and decided to come home.

RICK: And we saw it on Facebook that you were turning this town into the town of enactments and re-enactments and decided again that it was time to come home. It's good to be home mama.

ROXANA: All right, I'm so happy to have you back here, Multicolor wouldn't have been complete without my boys. And the rest is silence! Silence with words.

ALL THE CHARACTERS, ENACTERS AND RE-ENACTERS (*Singing together in a grand finale opera ending*): Sileeeeeeence! With Woooooords!

(End of Tableau X)

Tableau XI

The Beginning of the Play

Tour Guide dressed in Multicolor tuxedo is taking tourists on the Historic Tour of Small Southern Town turned into the Town of Multicolor. The year is 2030.

TOUR GUIDE: Hello everybody, welcome to the Historic Tour of the Town of Multicolor. This used to be The Town with Very Nice People or the Small Southern Town. We are moving right along. In our town we cared more about banks and churches than we cared about artists. We cared more about a couple of Confederate Generals and their stuffed horses than about the women and men who worked and created multicolored beauty. And then the town went empty, dead, it became a sorry, sad and racist little town with no imagination. The University was even worse than the town with its white men leaders holding on to the glory of the white race. Things got out of whack, stale, rotten. Businesses were dying out, souls were dying out, confederate re-enactors were roaming the streets in a craze waving confederate flags, women were humiliated in divorce and custody hearings or discriminated against at their workplace, blah, blah, blah. In short it was not the best place to live even though people would say crap like: "oh, it's such a nice place to raise your children!" But then this émigré writer Roxana Mincu had had enough of that crap and restructured our whole town. She made it into the town of enactments and reenactments and gave each corner in town a special purpose, creating new histories and new realities. Businesses came back to life, the street life came back to life, night life came back to life and we became unique in the world with our theatrical town that reenacts just about everything in the world there is to be acted and reenacted and by doing so creates new and unprecedented life. We are the number one most diverse town in the universe, that's why we are called the town of Multicolor which is the new diversity. Everything coexists and

- 122 -

transforms itself, nothing gets stale, nothing fades, we keep the colors alive and all mixed up, bold and vibrant. Yes, sure you can immigrate, find asylum, and settle in our town, the immigration process is easy. All you have to do is choose a corner or make a corner of your own and that gives you a share of the town, a portion of ownership. It's Marxist capitalism softened with performance art. It works, I tell you, everybody wants to come live here now, soon the whole world will want to come live here and then our town will take over the world and there you have it – we can say we made the world a better place.

The final and true END of the Play

House in a Boat with Food and No God.

A Nomadic Dystopia on Water

"This play is a great delight and highly entertaining! I am impressed with Radulescu's use of language and how she is introducing the world and its history. And the characters are completely delightful and feel authentic and necessary with needs of their own." **Emma-Goldman Sherman, award winning playwright, founder of 29th street Playwriting Collective.**

CHARACTERS (In order of appearance on stage):

NERMINA -   Worried mother from Poland tough, domineering, loving

SINISTRA - Daughter of NERMINA rebellious, sensuous, capricious

MAX   - A small boy in a boat and the son of GOD, playful, loving, courageous

TOMATO   - Child of NERMINA and MAX, smart, resourceful

POTATO   - Child of NERMINA and MAX, sassy, inquisitive

GODDESS   - Mother/Goddess of the earth that was killed and massacred by GOD. The parts of her body are spread throughout the ocean. She is larger than life, powerful, no-nonsense

PLASTIC BAG - Villain/Hero the leader of all plastic bags filling the oceans, cunning, treacherous, but with a sense of justice

ICE CREAM WOMAN - Lost daughter of GODDESS, sensuous, fragile

HOUSE IN A BOAT - The house carried in the boat that holds all the characters in their journey, moody, irritable

LOLA MINIATURE WOMAN IN A BOWL - Keeper of tears, of secrets and helper of lost travelers

VIVIAN GIANT WOMAN IN A TREE - Hostess of the Kingdom of GOD and helper of the group of travelers lead by NERMINA

GOD   - Vampire Leader of the world, usurper of freedoms, destroyer of the earth, ex-husband of GODDESS, belligerent, gross

DRACULA - Young man kept in captivity in Transylvania by GOD, sensitive, frail

SETTINGS

The action of this play takes place on water, under water, in the salt mines of Poland and in Dracula's castle in Transylvania. The mother daughter pair Nermina and Sinistra are in desperate search for food and give one last try to saving the world from total extinction. Since a large part of the play takes place on water or under water, it is up to the imagination of the director to create and suggest that environment, either by actually having water on stage or by projections of water, or a back drop, or by other staging strategies. Stage directions preceded by "Voice" should be uttered out loud either by a voice-over, or by a narrator-character on stage in epic theater style; or as if recounting a fairy-tale.

TIME

Indefinite time in the future, following the flooding of almost the entire earth surface by ocean water.

ACT I

Bottlecap Island and the Son of God

NERMINA: We are going in that direction ... In *that* direction, can't you hear?

SINISTRA: I can't turn the boat around mama, it's too late, you should have told me earlier.

NERMINA: You should have known better and rowed in the direction of the food smell.

SINISTRA: We can't turn the boat around, or we'll be eaten by sharks and plastic bags. We'll drown in algae and polymers and become amoebas all over again. We must keep moving forward, it's our only chance.

NERMINA: I'd rather be an amoeba than roam on these crazy waters all day and all night and all my life. I wish I had never left Poland. The bread was good, and we had land, not just water, water, water.

SINISTRA (*Rowing desperately as she is trying to reorient or change the direction of the boat.*): You forget how they started purging people like us, mama, you always forget the unpleasant details and idealize the few good ones. That's why we never get anywhere.

NERMINA: This time we will get somewhere for sure, I feel it everywhere in my body. Some place with earth and food. I can smell it. Our boat is depleted, and house is empty and doesn't want to talk anymore. All we have left to eat are a couple of rotten urchins and a Ziplock bag.

SINISTRA: We don't eat Ziplock bags mama, remember? They eat us. It's a cruel world out there. I'd rather drown than be eaten by a Ziploc bag.

NERMINA: Or a plastic bottle cap, ha, ha. (*She laughs so hard she shakes the boat*): You know, the plastic bottle caps that were never recycled, remember?

SINISTRA: Yes, of course I remember I was in fifth grade in our new American life in a small town in the South and one day they announced that plastic bottle caps were no longer going to be recycled. And I thought then, "Fuck it, what is going to happen with all those plastic bottle caps? One day the ocean will be covered by fucking plastic bottle caps from one end to the other." And here you are!

> *She points to an island of bottle caps on her left that she is trying to avoid in her rowing.*

NERMINA: You were cussing in your mind when you were in fifth grade? In English! Why weren't you cussing in Polish? What's wrong with Polish swear words? This is how people lose their heritage. Aha, that's how!

SINISTRA: Stop it mother. Of course, I was cussing in English, we had immigrated to America, remember, or have you forgotten that important episode of our lives? I was trying to fit in, assimilate, you know, all that crap. Plus, our school had surveillance cameras and listening devices that could read even your innermost thoughts. So, I didn't want them to know I was speaking another language.

NERMINA: Yea, right. For a second, I thought we had immigrated to Africa. That would have been better, you know. The food would have been better.

> *VOICE: Suddenly the boat loses control because of a big wave. Plastic Bag surges out of water howling and making terrifying sounds and gestures as if he were going to eat Sinistra and Nermina. The two women fight with it and try hard to keep their balance, so the boat does not turn over.*

NERMINA (*Shouting Polish swear words to Plastic Bag in a resounding voice then turning back to English*): Let go of the boat you cheap Walgreens Plastic Bag. I am a Polish chemist and I will turn you back to your original polymers in a second. I will disintegrate you until you will be nothing but a bunch of sorry polymeric particles, you motherfucking piece of second rate non-degradable under-degradable little shit! Get your hands off my daughter.

> VOICE: *Plastic Bag appears disoriented and taken aback, deflates himself and floats away. The boat has now moved and is floating successfully. Our two heroines have to stave off any enemies, any creatures that try to get ahead of them in the desperate search for food. It's a jungle out there.*

SINISTRA: Wow mama, I had no idea you still had it in you. Whatever! I can't figure out where the food smell is coming from. There is a crossroads of food smells right here, so when you say to row in the direction of the smell, I don't really know what that direction is.

NERMINA: You never had a sense of direction anyways!

SINISTRA: Food is direction, I go after the food smell. Do you ever have anything nice to say to me mama? Why do you always have to put me down in front of other people and Plastic Bag?

NERMINA: Just get over it, ok? You need to get you used to all the abuses you'll have to take as an immigrant Black Polish American, is all. So, go already. Follow one of the fucking smells, alright!

SINISTRA: All right, whatever you say. I'll go in the direction of the stewed tomato smell. I'm channeling a couple of smells and I choose the stewed tomato smell. It's an honest Polish smell. We are Black Polish people mama? I never knew that.

NERMINA: Yes, indeed we are Black Polish people. I never told you this, but we first immigrated from America to Poland because they were killing people like us everywhere. Poland had been my first home but I wanted to birth you on American soil so you could become president. You were born on an American farm if you want to know the full truth about your origins. That's where I met your father. On a farm in the South somewhere, boring as fucking hell. Until they started killing us. If you turned the wrong corner, bang! If you went into the wrong supermarket, bang! If you drove with your window open, bang!

So, your father and I decided to move somewhere in Eastern Europe where we had heard things were good again. We never told you this so you wouldn't feel out of place in Poland. But then they started getting crazy there too and they started killing people with their fucking kielbasa. Before you know it, they'll be throwing kielbasa at you. And then there was no more food so we re-immigrated to America on account of the food wars in Poland. By then all the people like us had disappeared in America. And then the food wars started in America too among the few people that had remained. So here we are sailing all day and all night and fighting with the Plastic Bags and killing ourselves to detect some food smells so we can survive on these freaky waters.

SINISTRA (*Completely shocked by her mother's revelations about her origins, she loses control of the boat and they end up capsizing in plastic bottle cap island*): Holy sauerkraut mama, why the fuck are you only telling me all this now? And where is my father? I thought I didn't have a father, I thought he was killed in a boating accident on the Baltic Sea when I was too little to remember.

NERMINA (*Acting as if she is not sure or hiding something*): That's right, he was, he was ... There is a time and a place for everything. Better focus on getting us out of this fucking bottle cap hell now before night falls. We are capsized in bottle caps, go figure!

SINISTRA: All right mama, but you owe me an explanation for all this and somehow, I don't really believe the story of the boating accident any longer.

> *Sinistra first eats everything that is left in the boat: algae, urchins, sea horses and the last of the Polish tomatoes, after which she pushes the oar into the bottle cap island.*

Help me mama, damn it, I'm trying to dismantle this damn bottle cap island so we can get through here. The least you could do after you lied to me my whole life about my father is help us get back on track. I'm starving, we have to get to the nearest food place, or I'll starve to death.

*Aggressive music suggesting destruction is heard as Sinistra and
Nermina are dismantling the bottle cap mountain island, which
suddenly turns into stellar eerie music like a liberation.*

NERMINA: Oh no, look Sinistra, look what's under the bottle cap: a
city of squash! Can you believe it, this is where they hid the yellow
foods, the bastards! A whole generation of people died in America
because of the lack of yellow foods. We thought they had all
disappeared, you know, like become fucking extinct.

SINISTRA: I know right? Goddamn beta-carotenes and shit, they
became protected species or something. I remember I was in third
grade and the civics teacher found a whole bunch of squashes and
carrots in little Jimmy's locker that he had hidden away for his family
who were all starving. The teacher got so mad, that he took his gun out
of his pocket and shot little Jimmy in the head, all on account of a
bunch of fucking carrots. "Anything but the carrots," he was yelling.
He was a fucking psychopath that civics teacher.

NERMINA: That was during the food wars my dear, America was a
poor country by then, they had to shoot the children who stole food,
particularly the yellow foods ...

SINISTRA: What are you talking about mother? "They had to shoot
the children?" Sometimes I wonder whether you are in your right
mind, I swear. I think your brain has all but dried up from hunger.
Here have some squash, it might help heal your cruel streak.

> *Nermina starts sobbing uncontrollably. Her sobs rock the boat
> so violently that the boat frees itself from the mound of bottle
> caps and starts floating through the mass of bottle caps that
> collapses around them.*

NERMINA: How can you talk like that to your mother and break your
mother's heart, and on account of carrots of all things?! You know I
would do anything for you and there is nothing I wouldn't do for you.
And you also know it's important for you to eat, or... you, you know ....

SINISTRA: (*She is rowing the boat through the walls of bottle caps and around the city of squash that is right in the center like an orange oasis*): That's what I call rocking the boat mama!

> *Nermina gathers a whole bunch of squash, yellow zucchini and carrots, puts them in the boat and peels them with her teeth and nails for her daughter.*

NERMINA: Here you are my love, please eat some of these wonderfully delicious tasting fresh yellow and orange food salad. It will, you know, make you strong and make you grow more.

SINISTRA: I'm already a grown woman, mama, I don't need to grow any more. What do you want me to be a giant? And this looks gross, I'd rather die than eat this shit. It even looks like shit. I can no longer live on the sea. I want to die, that's it.

> *VOICE: Max appears from behind the oasis of yellow vegetables in the middle of the dismantled island of plastic bottle caps. He is a delightful apparition, with dark complexion and curly black hair, and has the size of a zucchini squash, maybe ten inches tall and is rowing a tiny red boat shaped like a fish. As he gets closer, it becomes clear the boat is made of red plastic bottle caps.*

MAX: Hello dear ladies! Boy, am I happy to see you! I thought I'd never see any humans again and that I was going to die here on this deserted bottle cap and squash island all by myself. It just goes to show one should never lose hope until one is dead. And then it's ok to lose hope when you are dead.

NERMINA: Who the hell are you little man?

SINISTRA: Mother, I can't believe you just called this lovely visitor "little man." What the hell is going on with you today?

NERMINA: Well, he is little, isn't he! I am just worried about you, is all. You know you need to eat more before sunset. Worry about one's child turns one into a cruel person. It poisons your liver. I don't care about this little man coming out of squash and his hurt feelings. You must eat, or you'll die, that's all there is to it.

SINISTRA: Yea, all right whatever mother, here I'll eat some of this disgusting looking squash with some seawater to take away the squash taste...

> *Just when she is about to take a bite from the squash, Max jumps into her boat and she drops the food in the water. Nermina is getting more and more desperate and worried and pulls at her hair, leans over the edge of the boat, puts her head in the water and other acrobatics.*

NERMINA: Who are you? Where the hell did you come from little man?

MAX (*Happy to be paid attention to and talked to*): I am a remnant.

SINISTRA: A remnant of what?

MAX: A remnant of life on earth. My parents died in a boating accident and I went on to live with an uncle. He was a criminal and a cannibal and said he owed as much to my mother who was his sister: not to kill and not to eat me. But then he got tired of caring for me and threw me in the water. I am twenty years old, but I never grew bigger because of the plastic bottle caps. I survived for twenty years on sucking the remnants out of the bottle caps: remnants of peach nectar, soymilk, apple juice, coconut milk, chocolate milk, green tea, pomegranate juice, limeade, strawberry smoothie and rubbing alcohol.

SINISTRA: Mama, what's with everybody dying in boating accidents? How come his parents died in a boating accident just like you said my father died? And why the hell were you sucking rubbing alcohol out of the bottle caps?

MAX: I sucked on everything that I found but the rubbing alcohol kept me high and healthy, if you know what I mean.

> *He laughs heartily, shaking the boat hard despite his small size.*

SINISTRA: Watch out you, crazy nut, or we'll all end up in a boating accident.

She is weak and faint from lack of eating. Nermina starts crying again as she sees her daughter melt away from malnutrition.

NERMINA(*Changing tactics and being more cunning*): Sinistra, maybe you would like to offer our little guest some of this delicious squash I just prepared for you, he must be hungry after surviving on food remnants inside bottle caps for so long.

SINISTRA (*Gets caught in her mother's game and is offering some of her untouched squash and carrots meal to Max*): Oh here, here, here, have some of this if you can stand it. I think it's gross, but you know, *de gustibus*, as they say in Latin.

Max starts eating very daintily and as she is watching him, Sinistra becomes hungry and wants to eat some herself.

MAX: I'll go get some more squash from over there. Look how much squash and carrots are sitting in that net. The fishermen must have thought they were fishing and instead they caught themselves a whole bunch of yellow and orange foods. Look it here Miss Sinistra, have yourself this sweet soft squash.

SINISTRA (*She is fascinated by Max and his gentleness and starts eating greedily to her mother's great relief*): Max, I haven't enjoyed food like this in a long time, this is delicious. This squash tasted like shit the first time I tried it and now it tastes delicious. Mama I want to marry Max. I'm in love with him. He made me eat squash.

NERMINA: My daughter you have no coherence in your thoughts because of the prolonged starvation. You can't marry Max, he's too small for you. You'll never be able to have children. Besides, you lost all nourishment in your ovaries; you can no longer conceive.

MAX: I'm not so small Miss Nermina, I'm twenty-five years old and still growing by the minute. I want to marry Miss Sinistra too, I've waited for her my whole entire life sucking on bottle caps and drinking rubbing alcohol. There is no time to wait, now with everything that is happening, people live in a day what they used to live in a century. We'll give nourishment to Miss Sinistra's ovaries, and we'll repopulate the world, don't you worry Miss ...

NERMINA: Can you stop with all this Miss this and Miss that ...

SINISTRA: I like him calling me Miss, mama, I've never been called Miss and it makes me hungry when I hear it. Do you always have to criticize everything I do and like mama? This is my destiny, I know it now, Max is my destiny and I love it. I promise I'll eat every day from now on mama, even the disgusting squash, just give us your blessing, please!

NERMINA: All right, all right, have it your way. If Mr. Max here is going to keep you nourished and fat, that's good enough for me.

MAX: Thank you, Miss Nermina, I'll take good care of your daughter, I promise. She won't lack for anything.

> VOICE: Max is going through some strange contortions like seizures and suddenly a halo of light surrounds him. Uplifting choral music is heard from the bottom of the sea.

MAX: And that's because I am the son of God!

NERMINA: What did you say?

MAX: I said I am the son of God.

NERMINA: What the fuck! You are the son of God and you didn't tell us? And I thought your mother and father died in a boating accident!

MAX: Yes, that's right, they did, but they were just my terrestrial parents. They were Mafia. They were bad people who stole food from everybody so God my father sent them on a boat trip and there he killed them. He gave them to the Sharks who chewed them up and then God took charge of my education.

NERMINA: If you are the son of God, then how come you were starving there among the plastic bottle caps licking juices out of them and getting high on rubbing alcohol and not even able to feed yourself on the fucking squash all around you?

MAX: He wanted to test me, my dad wanted to see if I survived in the wilderness, if I was strong enough to be the son of God. So, I was passing the test quite well when I got so mad that my own father was putting me through hell, and letting the world be destroyed, that I killed him.

SINISTRA: What? You killed God your father?

MAX: Yes, I did, he was a mother fucker. I hated him. And after I killed him, he punished me for another ten years in bottle cap inferno. The squash is a new thing, it's only been here for a few days, it all arrived in the fishing net, I have no idea how. But by then I was already addicted to the bottle cap remnants and rubbing alcohol. You know how God the father is, no matter how many times you kill him, he keeps coming back up and punishing you. That's how boys get fucked up in the head and then they want to kill everybody. Plus, I missed my terrestrial mother Mitzi, she was a good woman even if she was Mafia. She did those Mafia things for me, to feed and raise me and nurse me. I want to bring her back to life and make her queen of the universe. Goddess of the universe. Now that I'm married to beautiful Miss Sinistra, I can go look for my mother and then I want to kill God once and for all.

NERMINA: Wait a minute! How are you going to get your mother back? I thought she was eaten by sharks. And no way am I giving my blessing for you to marry my daughter and carry her across the ocean looking for your food for sharks mother and trying to kill your father. You are a bad, bad boy. You are a bad son.

MAX: That's ok, goddesses are always massacred one way or another and then they come back to life if their child goes looking for their pieces to put them back together. You know, just like a puzzle. We'll go around asking all the Sharks if they saw and ate her and ask them to give her back. I'll put her remainders in this fishing net here and then I'll put them all back together. And we'll never lack food again. And Miss Sinistra will never lack food and she'll be healthy and fat and give birth to a beautiful ocean baby. I'll make her a royal house a bit farther down where there are no plastic bottle caps and no Plastic Bag! And you can come live with us Miss Nermina!

NERMINA: Oh thanks, that's kind of you. How come you are so small if you are the son of God?

> *Max starts crying profusely and jumps out of his red fish boat into Sinistra's arms like a baby. For a moment they make a mother and child pose.*

SINISTRA: Mama, can't you stop it with the questioning? Don't you see how you upset him? I don't care, I love him anyways, he's a baby husband, I like that. His strength does not lie in his size but in his spirit of rebellion. He and I can save the world together.

MAX: That's right, we'll save the world. And I'll grow some more with the help of Miss Sinistra's love. Didn't you know love makes you grow? Now I have to find my mom, and everything will be all right.

NERMINA: Fuck the world, it's not worth saving, let the bloody world die!

SINISTRA: All right mother, we are not going to listen to your retrograde and cynical view of the world. We are going to try finding all the foods and all the body parts of Max's mom Mitzi and save the world and make a better one. Isn't that right, Max?

PLASTIC BAG (*Who surges out of the water and tries overturning the boat*): Like hell you will. The world is kaput! Done! I dominate the world now and you are nothing, but a bunch of freaks and pretentious motherfuckers and I will eat you all for breakfast in one gulp.

> *VOICE: Plastic Bag opens a huge mouth that is larger than the entire boat with the House in it and tries swallowing it. At that point Sinistra and Max start making passionate love which*

fascinates Plastic Bag and distracts him. His mouth closes. He becomes lascivious and loses interest in the boat and the people in it. Nermina takes over the boat and rows out of the bottle cap and squash area oasis.

NERMINA: If we weren't in this very unusual situation of almost being eaten by a Plastic Bag spelled with capital letters, I would say it's indecent for you two to be copulating in public and in front of your mother. But given the life and death, end of the world kind of predicament we are in, I let it be. After all what the hell, make love not war, right? At least I hope it's going to be productive. Shouldn't you go inside the House to make your baby though? Why the hell have I gotten myself ruined paying the fucking mortgage for the House In Boat, if you can't even make a baby inside it?

Sinistra stops the copulation, picks up Max lovingly and runs with him inside the house.

NERMINA (*Rowing vigorously*): Kids! What are you going to do! Kids are kids, they never listen to you. And then kids make other kids and on and on, the never-ending story of fucking up the world.

Lively sounds of romping, playing, and copulating are heard from inside the tiny House inside the boat. Then a silence follows and then the sounds of a baby crying. Sinistra and Max come out of the House each holding a baby. One is a tiny baby the size of a thumb and resembling a Potato, the other is a Tomato baby of the same size. Nermina is shocked but she must keep rowing to get them as far as possible from Plastic Bag.

NERMINA: You gave birth to a tomato?

SINISTRA: Yes mother, these days we must give birth to the food for the baby at the same time as the baby. It's a new reproductive technique I learned about in family education class in Poland. They didn't teach us anything useful in American family education class, they only taught us about guns, but thank God I remembered my Polish upbringing at the last minute.

NERMINA (*More and more puzzled*): You are going to make food of one of your babies? I'm glad I lived to see this one too.

SINISTRA: No mama, seriously, what do you think we are, cannibals? This is a special baby Tomato that produces other baby tomatoes for consumption. It's a new food chain. She will feed her sister; she specializes in heirloom cherry tomatoes. Families must be self-sufficient nowadays and produce their own foods. Our babies are twins but not identical twins as you well can see. We'll call the tomato baby Tomato and the other one Potato. Because Max is the son of God, we can make babies from the nightshade family. Once he finds his mother, we'll be able to make babies from other families like the cucurbits and the cruciferous ones. We'll have watermelons and cabbage and cauliflower again. This is how we save the world. I told you it was a good idea for me to marry Max. Plus, you see how now that he's discovered his masculinity, he has grown a bit taller, hasn't he?

NERMINA: Like hell he did. He's still as tiny as Tom fucking Thumb. A great family you will be, you two, with children who are called Tomato and Potato. And let me ask you this: if Tomato is going to feed Potato, then who is going to feed Tomato?

SINISTRA: TOMATO will feed herself; she is a self-sufficient parthenogenetic child. It's the way of the future mama.

NERMINA: I see. Interesting! Oh, what the hell we are all family! At least we got rid of Plastic Bag and are sailing on clear waters. Welcome to our family Max. Now go help your wife clean House after all the mess you made copulating and making Tomato and Potato. And let's go find some sharks with Goddess body parts in their stomachs!

> VOICE: *Night falls and a glorious violet darkness envelops the sea and the boat, with orange stars flickering in the sky. A celestial music of the stars is heard, Sinistra and Max are*

lovingly holding one baby each, sleeping next to each other on a bed of protected jelly fish and red algae, while Nermina is sleeping at the oar, ready to start moving at a moment's notice in case of danger.

End of Act I

(Blackout)

ACT II

Reconstructing the Goddess

VOICE: The children Tomato and Potato dance with each other on the water, Sinistra and Max dance together on the water and Nermina dances with Plastic Bag. The light is eerie, violet, the music is heartbreak sentimental, accordion and violin.

SINISTRA: See mama, how we can all walk and dance on water? It's all because I'm married to the son of God. And the miracles haven't even started. Wait till we find his mom, the big Miss Goddess of the universe who was massacred to pieces by God the Father and by the American media and by Plastic Bag. And who also died in a boating accident. Everybody had a part in killing the Goddess. And mom, why were you dancing with Plastic Bag just now? He is a rapist and a murderer. What got into you?

NERMINA: Oh, calm down my daughter. He apologized. He was transformed after he saw you and Max making your babies. He masturbated and then he wanted to commit suicide. He was humanized. And he decided to self-destruct to help us save the world. He is going to lead the Plastic Bags suicide squad across the ocean. You can do wonders with kindness and a sexy dance.

MAX (*Interrupts the dance feverishly and makes everybody slide on water and back inside the boat. He is crying*): I miss my mama! Why did Dad have to kill her? I'm glad I killed the bastard. I am not sorry that I committed patricide. Now we can all go look for mom! I lied about it. Mitzi is my real mom, both human and Goddess, she just wanted to live like a normal Mafia person to give me a normal life and interact with other Mafia children. Let's go look for mom. It will be so much fun.

> *Everybody sings hooray and claps cheerfully. They put on scuba diving suits and large oxygen masks; the next scene happens under water with scuba masks.*

NERMINA: There are so many sharks down here, how are we supposed to know which ones have eaten the Goddess and which ones haven't? And by the way what's the real name of this Goddess? I need to know who I'm looking for.

MAX: Miss Nermina ...

NERMINA: If you call me Miss Nermina one more time, I'll strangle you and send you to the Sharks to meet your mother.

> *Max starts crying hysterically, large red bubbles come out of his scuba mask. Colored fish and sharks start circling around him as if ready to eat him. Sinistra protects him with her body and carries him in her arms like a baby farther away from the large school of fish. Water fluid music can be heard.*

SINISTRA: I hate you mama. Look what you've done. You scare and traumatize him all the time. You are going to kill him and if you do that, I'll kill myself and then I'll kill you. Bitch!

NERMINA: How come he's so fragile if he's the son of God? And what do you mean by killing him? If he's the son of God, isn't he immortal?

TOMATO and POTATO (*Who by now have grown into teenagers are interfering in a chorus*): Shut the fuck up everybody and start looking for Goddess. Look for the fat lazy sharks, those are the ones who ate her. And by the way, the name of the Goddess is Violeta not Mitzi. What kind of a Goddess name is Mitzi? She was once a flower and then a mushroom and then an enormous woman with a hundred vaginas and right now she's food for sharks. This Goddess was one sexy mama!

MAX: That's right children she was your grandmama and the mother of all the universe. She gave birth to me through all her one hundred vaginas.

> *Sinistra gets on top of one of the fat sharks with a knife and is ready to slice him open, but Max stops her.*

MAX: No, no, no, we don't kill the Sharks, we talk to them and make them consent to vomiting back the body parts of Mama Violet that they have swallowed. It must be consensual and non-violent. Sharks and these little colored fish are the only ones left in the whole worldwide ocean. The feistiest ones survived, the military fish, they fought Plastic Bag and Bottle Caps with a vengeance until they withdrew. The Scissors Tail Sargent fish, the Major Fish, the Japan Surgeon Fish, the Arabian Surgeon Fish, you know, the Asian ones. So be gentle, they won't hurt you.

> VOICE: All the characters go after fat sharks and manage to make them give back the Goddess parts that they had swallowed. There is a lot of commotion, waves, and bubbles. They get almost all the parts except for one.

MAX: Now we all have to put her parts together in the correct order.

SINISTRA: Max, but we are missing her heart. We need her heart; how is she going to live and rule the world without a heart?

MAX: She's got vaginas, a hundred of them. And she's got a huge brain. Here it is – I got it from the belly of an Angel shark. His belly was going to explode.

NERMINA: All right so let's worry about the heart later and put together what we've got so far – a hundred vaginas, every bit of every one of them, a hundred-pound brain, arms, legs, boobs, eyes, nose, earring, intuition and nail polish. She's got pretty nails this one.

> They all go up to the surface carrying the Goddess body parts, hauling them into the boat. Max tenderly embraces her body parts crying over them. Sad music.

TOMATO and POTATO: Mama, we know where the Goddess heart is, we had a dream before we were born. She told us to look for her heart in a castle in Transylvania. That's where God the Father and the Vampire hid it from the world.

SINISTRA: God the father is a vampire? Max why didn't you tell me?

MAX: I thought you knew, I thought everybody knew that God the Father is a fucking vampire. Why do you think I killed him? Yes, God the Father is a vampire born in America who immigrated to Transylvania after he sucked everybody's blood in his native country. Once in Transylvania he went about his vampire ways and started sucking everybody's blood over there and taught everybody how to do it too. It's the opposite of what people think about the big Dracula in Transylvania and all that crap. He was let into the country as a legal and before they knew it, he was wreaking havoc everywhere in Eastern Europe too. It goes to show that it's the legals who are the most dangerous, they go right under your skin and suck you dry. He led the movement for environmental collapse and made himself a huge palace of plastic bags and plastic bottles and threw all the caps in the ocean. My mom begged him to stop all that nonsense and tried to protect the ocean with her own body. That's when he killed and butchered her and threw her parts into the ocean. But I never knew he put her heart inside the vampire castle in Transylvania. I should have thought of it! That's why you have children, they give you invaluable information from their intrauterine dreams.

NERMINA: God doesn't have ethnic origins. I have never heard such nonsense. God is universal.

MAX: That's what people think, that's what the government wants you to think, but in fact God is a racist pig.

SINISTRA: MAX don't talk like that in front of the children, still, he is their grandfather.

MAX: They must know the truth.

TOMATO: Mama, what does guberment mean?

POTATO: It's government, not guberment, stupid. Didn't they teach you anything in intrauterine school?

NERMINA: Children, stop fighting with each other. This is how wars are started and how the world goes to hell. Government, children, is a group of horny men who want to destroy the world and fuck everybody in the ass.

SINISTRA: I can't believe the kind of crap you are teaching your grandchildren. Max and I are trying to teach our children critical thinking and tolerance and you are putting all this hateful stuff in their little bulbous heads. They can argue all they want as long as they don't kill each other on account of their differences. Isn't that true? Look at them how cute they are, I could just eat them up. As a matter of fact ...

She turns ferocious and acts as if she is tempted to eat Tomato and Potato.

NERMINA (*Grabbing her and trying to stop her from eating her children with Max's help*): Quick, she's way past her eating time, give her something to eat, just not her children. Thank Goddess her appetite is back though. The fresh seawater helped.

Tomato produces a bowlful of cherry tomatoes, and hands them to her mother to eat. Sinistra eats them voraciously and calms down.

MAX: See the advantage of creating parthenogenetic children; you never grow short of food. Well, almost never ...

SINISTRA: Max, how did you kill your dad?

MAX: There is no time for that now, we have to put mom back together and then go find her heart in the Transylvanian castle.

TOMATO and POTATO: Yay, we are going on a trip to see grandpa's castle. Mom, can we suck somebody's blood when we get there?

MAX: Absolutely not! No blood sucking ever. People are nice and hospitable over there, you know, you can't just go into their country and start sucking their blood.

SINISTRA: Why not? Isn't that what your father did?

MAX: My dear love, you can't do it because it's not done anymore, my father was old fashioned.

SINISTRA: And where did you hide *his* body, you little monster?

NERMINA: We don't have time for all your stupid philosophical arguments, we have to go before Violeta the Goddess dies a second time or the hundredth and last time. Let's finish putting her back together and let's get on the road, shall we?

> *VOICE: Great commotion as all the characters are working to put together the body of the Goddess, like building a Lego creature or putting together a puzzle. They finish the body with the hundred vaginas and the giant head, but a big hole in the place of the heart. It looks both grotesque and unexpectedly beautiful. Glorious uplifting music with humorous playful but also dark tones.*

SINISTRA: There you go, we did it you all! Teamwork what can I say. Good job children, one day you'll be presidents of Poland America and the Arab world all in one. You'll live and rule from a submarine.

MAX: That's right, your mother speaks the truth. But now we must go to Transylvania to find Violeta's heart. Bless her heart.

> *He laughs, proud of his own pun. Also, Max has grown a bit bigger in the process of Goddess reconstruction.*

And once we find her heart, I tell you what ...

TOMATO and POTATO: What daddy, what? Tell us! That was so much fun building the Goddess. Can we unmake her and make her again?

MAX: Absolutely not! This was not a rehearsal; it was the real thing. And guess what, once we find my mom's heart, your Daddy will grow by a foot or two. Daddy never grew up properly because he didn't have enough food and he didn't have his mommy like you two are lucky to have her. So, take care of your mommy here, live and learn, never kill your mom or your wife. Promise?

TOMATO and POTATO: Yes, we promise daddy. We'll only kill mom if she's mean. And we'll kill you too daddy if you are mean and don't give us candy. Can we have a wife too?

MAX: Sure, wait till you get to Transylvania, there are lots of beautiful women there to choose from. Some are prostitutes. And the tomatoes are all home grown. And the candy is delicious. Maybe we'll immigrate to Transylvania, who knows. Hm? What do you think beloved SINISTRA?

TOMATO: Mama, what's a prostitute?

SINISTRA: A prostitute is ....

The boat starts shaking violently and the Goddess is roaring.

GODDESS: Stop the talk and go to Transylvania already or I'll throw you all in the waves and make you food for sharks, ha, ha, ha ...

Atrocious laughter, then heartbreaking sobs.

MAX (*Starts crying and jumps into the arms of the Goddess*): Mama, mama, you are alive even without a heart. I missed you so much. I never thought I'll get to see you again after daddy killed you. You know I killed the bastard, don't you! Aren't you proud of your son? Mama, everybody lives on water now since you were killed and there is no food anymore. We have to eat our children now. But if we make it to Transylvania and get your heart from God the Vampire's castle, you'll make food again, won't you? And maybe some of the waters will withdraw back to their original sizes and we'll have some of the old earth back. We love our children, we don't want to eat them, but we might have to if we have no choice. Come over here kids and say hello to your grandma. Here mom, here are your grand kids, Tomato and Potato. They are asexual parthenogenetic children; they can feed themselves out of their own bodies as long as we keep them watered. No problem there, since we live on water now, ha, ha, ha!

TOMATO: Grandma why do you have so many vaginas? They are ugly.

GODDESS: So I can eat you better with them, ha, ha, ha. Gee but you two children are ugly. Why did you make such ugly children son?

SINISTRA: They are not ugly, they are vegetables, they are good kids, you just have to get used to them. Plus, they feed themselves, that's a real plus. And they know where your asshole husband hid your heart.

Turning to MAX and whispering.

I can't believe how mean and prejudiced your mama is. She is a vegetablist. Maybe your dad was right to kill the bitch.

MAX: Don't mind her my love, she doesn't know what she's talking about, she doesn't have her heart, remember? She is just thinking through her hundred vaginas, that's all.

NERMINA: I'm tired of listening to all this nonsense and sexist and vegetablist crap. Goddess has a brain, remember, she isn't just thinking with her vaginas. And if she did, she's got more brains in her vaginas than you have in your own brains. You are as stupid as your father. I can't believe my daughter married you when she could have married a good old Polish Mafia aristocrat with a normal size.

SINISTRA(*Attacks her mother furiously, pulls her hair, the boat is shaking, the House in the Boat is rattling and from it comes Ice Cream Woman with Pinwheel, looking as if she's just woken up*): I am going to kill you, you stupid bitch, you never loved me, you only love squash. I am only a pretext for you to gorge on disgusting squash. You always put me down, you always ....

ICE CREAM WOMAN: You need to calm down you all, or I'll suicide everybody out of existence. Stop fighting with each other you bunch of nasty morons, son of God and all. Some son of God you are! The son of God should sacrifice himself for humankind, not copulate with commoner women to produce a bunch of ugly veggies!

TOMATO and POTATO (*Crying profusely and hiding behind their mother*): Mama, why is everybody calling us ugly, why did you bring us into the world? We are going to kill ourselves, there!

They try to strangle each other.

ICE CREAM WOMAN (*Getting in between them and separating them*): Oh, come to mama, I was just playing with you to toughen your skins a bit. Life at sea is hard, and the world is mean, better to hear it from auntie Ice Cream than from strangers. Come on everybody, you all need to calm down and focus on your goal. You are beautiful pudgy tasty kids. Your goal is to get the heart of the goddess from Transylvania, after that you can kill each other all you want. Come on start licking me, you all look like you need some sweet caramel parsnip ice cream to calm down your hunger and murderous impulses.

> *Everybody starts licking Ice Cream Woman while she is moaning and gyrating like she's having an orgasm. A deep calm follows during which only the sound of the waves is heard, followed by a transcendent moment with elevated operatic mystical sounding music in which all the characters look transfigured. Silence, music, silence, music.*

SINISTRA (*Talking as if still in a trance*): I had a dream with aubergines and lollipops, with mushroom stew and artichokes. The polenta was dancing with the arugula in a dance hall in the salt mines of Poland.

MAX: What a coincidence, I too dreamed of the salt mines of Poland. They might be our only salvation, the place where food never ends, and all the chandeliers are made of salt crystals. We should make a detour to the salt mines on our way to Transylvania. I always said it that food and salvation will come from that part of the world.

POTATO: Mama, are we Noah's Ark?

NERMINA: What do you know! Did they teach you about Noah's Ark in intrauterine school too? No, we are not freaking Noah's Ark.

That's a different story. It's not our story. We don't believe in that story, it's not true, it's just a fairy tale.

MAX: Like hell we don't. Then how come I'm the son of God? If the Ark of Noah isn't true than I'm not true either.

NERMINA: Exactly my point. You are an impostor and God is an impostor.

SINISTRA: There you go again undermining me and my husband in front of the children.

GODDESS (*Roaring with anger, thundering with rage so that the boat and the House in it are shaking almost to breaking point and lightening is seen in the sky*): God *is* an Imposter. He not only killed me, but he killed all my children. Why the hell do you think I have a hundred freaking vaginas? I tried to keep up with his massacres so every time he killed one of my children, I grew another vagina and birthed another child, but he killed faster than I birthed. And in the end only Max remained. I hid him inside a bottle and sent him to the bottle cap island. Max is not an impostor; he is the real thing because he is the son of Goddess. Everything that came out of me is real. And then God killed me and dismembered me. By that time, I had no feeling left in my heart and didn't care about what he was doing to me. That's why it was so easy to just carve my heart out of me and send it to this remote place in Transylvania.

> *As she is speaking her roars turn to pained hoarse whispers, then she cries softly. Everybody cries. House also cries, Ice Cream Woman cries, a chorus of cries rises to the skies and becomes heartbreakingly melodious.*

ICE CREAM WOMAN: Mama, mama, I also survived the massacre. I am Max's Twin Sister, I was so tiny at birth that you didn't notice me mama, you were too stricken with grief. I hid inside the cupboard of an old lady in New Orleans and made myself into Ice Cream. That's how I survived the floods. And then I saw this pretty little House in this pretty little boat during the flood and I thought I'd hide inside it and wait and see what happens. And then Nermina and Sinistra jumped on board, killed the Somalian pirates and started navigating in search of food. That's my story. It's a true story.

NERMINA (*Talking in a southern accent*): You are from New Orleans too Ice Cream Woman? What a coincidence. So are we! Everybody's related to everybody else, what a miracle!

SINISTRA: We are? Since when are we also from New Orleans? What else are you hiding from me mama?

NERMINA: I don't know daughter, lots of many other things I guess, my memory is all jumbled up since the concussions I got from the Somalian pirates and the food wars in Poland and the new food wars in America and all the other crap I've been through. It's a wonder I remember anything at all in the chaos we've been living for so long. Just make your own story if you don't like the ones I'm telling you and give me a fucking break. It's a free ocean.

GODDESS (*She smiles and tries to kiss Ice Cream Woman who moves in an awkward way. Sad joyous music of recognition. Mother and daughter embrace awkwardly without words. Ice Cream Woman is dripping bits of herself in the mouth of Goddess*): My daughter, what a miracle, all is not lost then, the hole in my heart feels a little less empty! And you are delicious. Don't worry I won't eat you like your dad would have done. And what a brave and ingenious girl you are too, making yourself into Ice Cream Woman and surviving floods and pirates and governments. I guess one has to be edible to survive these days. In my time you had to make food, now you have to be food. What a world! Well let's not lose hope, you all get started towards that Transylvania castle and get my heart from out of there and I promise things will get better. We'll grow sea onions and watermelons and bring back the red foxes and the kumquats. This ain't Noah's freaking Ark, he just put a bunch of creatures in his boat and sailed on, we are making everything all over again out of seawater. It figures we have to work ten times harder than he did and get paid half the money since we are women and he was a man and you need one hundred vaginas to make up for one small dick.

SINISTRA: All right everybody, hold on to your seats I'm turning the boat over towards Transylvania via the salt mines of Poland. Ready?

ALL: Yes, ready let's go get that heart from the hands of the Vampire King God with a small penis.

> *Sinistra rows vigorously and they all sway following the movements of her rowing, laughing and singing.*

(End of Act II)

ACT III

VOICE: The boat with the entire group of characters is sailing across wavy seas, smooth seas, stormy seas, with them taking turns rowing. They are tired and hungry, the children are crying and Sinistra is famished, getting weaker and more deathly looking as time goes by, to her mother's desperation. The cherry tomatoes produced by Tomato are no longer enough and she has eaten the last of the urchins. Ice Cream Woman is also depleted, she can no longer give of herself to the crew, or she will disappear. Goddess has given birth to a handful of mushrooms through one of her vaginas, but she is also too weak to give birth to anything else without a heart. Everybody is at the end of their wits and strength. Suddenly a huge Plastic Bag comes out from the deep and pulls the entire boat to the bottom of the ocean.

SINISTRA (*As she is going down with the boat*): Bye children, bye Max, bye mom, I love you all so much, I guess here ends our big adventure on the sea to save the world. We tried.

GODDESS (*Who can talk under water because she is Goddess):* Shut up you all! Look, look over there. What do you see over there? Look how beautiful! Surprise!

PLASTIC BAG (*Handing out oxygen masks to everybody):* Here you have it you bunch of asshole losers. Didn't I tell you I was leading the anti-anti-environmental movement across the ocean? Why didn't you wait to work together with all my brothers, sisters, and Bottle Cap King before you decided to go off on your own? Didn't they teach you anything about diplomacy and collaboration in those plastic schools of yours?

NERMINA(*Speaks through the oxygen masks, the voice resonates through the deep and makes bubbles*):We didn't know you were, you know, on our side, environmentalists and what have you... we didn't think you cared.

PLASTIC BAG: What have I? What side? What viromonumentalists the hell are you talking about? Our species doesn't want to cohabit-ate with you bunch of asshole humans any longer, you created us and then overcrowded and multiplied us and made us indisfuckingtructible like a bunch of psycho idiots and threw us into the oceans and overheated every bit of every part of the earth with your fucking cars and disgusting hamburgers and marshmallows. We are all on suicide squad now, suicide bombing ourselves because of your greed. Serves you right you imbeciles that you have nothing to eat but your own shit and not even that because if you don't eat you don't shit, so you can't even eat shit, ha, ha, ha!

Thunderous laughter of Plastic Bag

TOMATO and POTATO (*They start crying in their oxygen masks*): Mr. Plastic Bag, please don't get mad at us and suicide bomb us, it's not our fault that our parents and grandparents are a bunch of cretins and destroyed everything. We are sustainable and parthenogenetic; we create our own food. We are a new generation.

TOMATO: Well I mostly create the food for myself, my twin sister and the rest of my family. Here taste a cherry Tomato! Please, give us another chance. Our Dad is the son of God and wants to make everything right again and we are going to find the heart of Goddess our grandmother and make her happy and productive again. We are going to ...

PLASTIC BAG: Shut up you whiny stupid children.

> *Eating the cherry tomatoes and enjoying it, becoming kinder and calmer.*

Not bad, not bad at all. Hey, say, isn't the bitch over there the same one who whooped my ass only a few days ago?

POTATO: Yes, she is Mr. Plastic Bag, she is grandma Nermina. We love her so much. She is strong and a chemist. She knows your composition and can bring you to your polymeric origins, so you don't have to suicide bomb yourselves. You can start over.

PLASTIC BAG: We don't fucking want to start over, you idiots, we want to be done, finished, kaput. We want the peace of a total and complete polymeric annihilation. That would be awesome. Plus, it's chemists like her that created us in the first place, ha, ha, they created their own destruction, stupid assholes.

POTATO: Don't you dare call our grandma bad names or I'll puncture your ass and make you into a Potato bag before you can say Tomato.

SINISTRA: Well said my daughter, we are so proud of you and your rebellious courage.

TOMATO: Mr. Plastic Bag, are you a boy or a girl, do you have a penis or a vagina?

PLASTIC BAG: I have neither of those things, you moron, I'm a fucking plastic bag.

POTATO: Well, then how come you can talk and have a mouth and are doing suicide bombs?

PLASTIC BAG: Hmm, good point! I don't know man, I guess our species has just evolved to be more like people while you people have devolved to the life of Plastic Bags.

POTATO: My sister and I are not people; we are vegetable humanoids. Our parents are human though. Sort of!

PLASTIC BAG: There you have it, I rest my case. Enough talk now, and let's get to action. Do you want to get to Transylvania and recover the heart of Goddess or what?

ALL (*Excitedly making bubbles through oxygen masks*): Yay, yay, let's go get grandma's heart.

MAX: By way of Polish salt mines, right? I want to know my wife's heritage and I heard the salt mines are the only part of Poland that survived. They were created by a Polish princess. Also, my wife craves for salt like a bitch, she needs to lick some of those salt mines, or she'll die. Please Plastic Bag, I'll owe you one! I'm exhausted, she wants to eat me like a praying mantis, besides wanting sex sixty-six times a day. My penis is all raw and limp. I guess sex calms her hunger for food.

PLASTIC BAG: Yea, all right, whatever, anything for the son of God! You shouldn't have married a fucking nymphomaniac eating machine.

MAX: Who are you calling nymphomaniac, hum, hm, I'll, I'll ...

Ready to jump at Plastic Bag and hurt him.

HOUSE IN A BOAT *(Starts shaking violently, howling, spewing dark smoke, tar, mixed with sea creatures, earth creatures, afterbirth, regurgitated foods, as well as a delirious barrage of words and sentences of doom and anger, the collective subconscious of angry humankind)*: Shut up you all of you despicable refuse of humanity aquatic nautical remnants degraded cud of the bottoms of the oceans flooded toilets sewage and margarine cold pressed in the Amazon jungle torn to pieces hunks of beef rotting in sun dried fly excrement be doomed to eternal submarine Mafia no algae no algae left only red Exxon Shell at least some oyster marmalade waiting for the second coming of Nelson Mandela in these times of national repercussions we pray for the souls of the dead and their asses to burn to ashes in the Red Sea of Israel in the name of the father and the holy moussaka just like mama used to make we pray for the souls of the yellow variety of vegetables and a woman's role is to make Mongolia great again until our father who art in heaven and Genghis Han the conqueror of three peas in a pod you too can do it, the south will rise again and the north and the east and the carrot pudding side effects include diarrhea and decapitation without anesthesia live in the present breathe deeply and die, die, die trade agreement in the ass in the ass macaroni and cheese family values and Salam Bombay. *(Stops abruptly.)* You guys, wouldn't happen to have a cigarette, would you?

All the characters are petrified and terrified, unmoved, barely breathing behind their oxygen masks.

SINISTRA (*Recovering from the shock, matter of fact*): Yes, House in a Boat does that sometimes when she is overly tired and has PMS and the food is gone. It makes her feel better, don't worry, she doesn't mean any harm, she's all words and no action.

PLASTIC BAG: Here House, take this cigarette here, it's my last one, I've been trying to quit forever. You deserve it after all you've been through. Just don't put yourself on fire, all right? Ha, ha, ha!

> *VOICE: The aquatic convoy advances in silence for a while, passing through underwater cities, lands, countries, mountains, the Eiffel Tower, the Empire State Building, a haystack with a needle in it, the Taj Mahal, the leaning tower of Pisa, the baseball hall of fame, the Hungarian Embassy in Burkina Faso, all of humanity stretching out in disarray at the bottom of the ocean.*

TOMATO and POTATO: Mom, Dad, can we please see the Eiffel Tower? We learned about it in intrauterine school.

GODDESS: We'll stop on the way back children we don't have time now, we must get to my heart before I die one more time and forever and your mom needs to lick some salt in those Polish mines before she dies of desalination. So, stop whining for now and shut the hell up.

> *VOICE: The aquatic convoy finally arrives at the entrance of the salt mines. They sail their way through many labyrinthine canals until they arrive at the salt mine ball room, an enormous hall with chandeliers made of salt crystals, statues made of salt, mirrors, everything is grandiose. A waltz is playing and couples in ballgowns and tuxedos as if from a different era are dancing, on the shiny salt floors as if in a dream. The group of characters are stunned.*

GODDESS (*Large tears falling on her face*): There was a time.... there was a time when all this was real, was how people lived. These people got stuck in their moment of happiness forever. They slipped through a crack in time. Don't get too close, don't speak loudly or it will all disappear. They are two hundred years old. They are survivors, you know, from Krakow, they survived the ... you know .... I loved them .... I protected them and granted them their wish of freezing them in their happiest moment.

> *Sinistra is oblivious to the dancing people and is licking the floors, the walls are all made of salt. Everybody else is watching in a state of enchantment.*

MAX: SINISTRA my love, we would have been so happy living at that time and dancing all day long. We would have been spared the oceans filled with all the grossness of humanity. We would have danced under salt chandeliers all lifelong.

SINISTRA: How boring. You call that life?

MAX: You call *this* life?

ICE CREAM WOMAN: Finally, a place where the temperature is constant and I'm not melting. I could get used to that.

TOMATO: Mama, Potato and I learned how to dance like that in intrauterine school. And we had sex with each other in intrauterine school too.

SINISTRA: What? You are incestuous twins? What have I done to deserve my crappy life and a bunch of monster vegetable children?

POTATO: We are not monster children mama, we are good self-sufficient children. We even got our PhD in intrauterine school. You made us mama, now you have to own us! Bitch!

MAX: Shut up children, respect your mother.

> *To SINISTRA, romantically.*

May I have this dance my love? Dancing is believing. I believe in you and you believe in me.

SINISTRA(*Shyly*): I don't know Max, not in front of the children! And I can't dance the waltz, I can only dance the boom, boom.

ICE CREAM WOMAN: Go woman, dance with your husband, it's now or never! Don't worry about the children, they had sex with each other in uterus for fuck's sake, they are not going to mind seeing you two dance. It's good for them to see their parents are human too.

HOUSE IN A BOAT: I order you to dance the boom boom and the malagueña or I'll collapse over all of you discombobulated fatherfuckers. I am your refuge and your home, space home, the one and only one you've got in the universe. What good am I if you don't dance in me? A House without dancing is like a wedding without a harpsichord. A House without a harpsichord is like a wedding without a House. It's now or never.

> *Sinistra and Max dance a slow languid dance, a now or never kind of dance with Sinistra holding Max in her arms like a baby. They cry and laugh and sing at the same time.*

POTATO: Isn't our mother so beautiful when she dances with Dad? She's like a rhubarb pie.

TOMATO: I don't know, I like our father more. He is gentler and he is tiny. And he's the one with the penis. That's what matters.

POTATO: I can't believe you are so sexist. You shouldn't talk about our father's penis, it's forbidden, didn't you know that? You are so stupid and ignorant Tomato! I'll squish you and make you Tomato juice. Let's see how you'll talk about dad's penis then.

TOMATO: Oh yea? And how about when you talked about our mother's vagina and said it reminded you of the insides of a ripe pumpkin?

POTATO: That's right, our mother's vagina is sacred, we came out of it. And all sacred things look like food and all food looks like sacred things and vice versa.

GODDESS: Everybody, take this moment in before we move on! There will never be another moment like this, I promise you. Sinistra and her husband Max are making history with their dance. They are dancing in times of apocalypse and that's what is going to save our planet. This tiny bitty love dance between the son of God and Goddess and the daughter of a chemist. Science and religion together. Too bad his father and I are divorced.

NERMINA: That's all right Goddess, forget the asshole of your husband, look at the state he left the world in and how well your children and grandchildren are doing without God the father. He was such a nuisance! He always cheated on you and spoke badly about you behind your back with his drinking buddies and now he's probably screwing some Transylvanian vampire whore on top of a big trash pile. Plus, he killed your children, massacred and dismembered you, remember? What the hell is wrong with you that you can't remember?

GODDESS: Because I don't have a heart, that's why, all my memories are in my heart, all my will is in my head. The heart/mind dichotomy, don't you know that?

POTATO: The dick what? Ha, ha, grandma said "dick."

MAX (*Cuddling in Sinistra's arms as they dance and whispering so the others don't hear*): I would sort of want to stay here, you know, forever. Ask for political asylum in this moment of dance. What do you think my love, should we just sneak into the forever dance moment of these people? Then we won't have to travel all the way to fucking Transylvania to get mother's heart. I grew up on a pile of fucking bottle caps, I wouldn't mind spending the rest of eternity with you dancing under salt crystal chandeliers. What do you say? It only takes one step. One waltz step and we're in paradise forever.

SINISTRA: I don't know Max, my love. What would happen to our children? I can't leave my children alone at the bottom of the ocean. They'll be eaten alive. Remember, they are Potato and Tomato. And I'll get so bored going around and round here for the rest of eternity. It was fun for a few minutes, but I'll go mad if I have to do this forever. We need to give one more try to saving the world. We must, we owe it to everybody, to ourselves, to Ice Cream Woman and Plastic Bag. They all counted on us.

MAX: All right, but if it doesn't work out and we can't save the world one last time, will you come and live here with me? Inside the dance moment? Promise?

SINISTRA: Yea, all right, promise. Let's go now.

> *VOIS: Sinistra and Max make one wrong step towards the moment of eternal waltzing bubble and the time bubble bursts. All dancers turn to dust instantaneously and disappear. Goddess cries profusely and tears at her hair.*

SINISTRA: See, what did I tell you? It was all fake, an illusion. A memory hologram. That's no place for us to take refuge to while we're still alive. These salt mines are spooked, let's get the hell out of here. I'm starving.

POTATO and TOMATO: Mom, Dad, why did you destroy the dancing people? They were so pretty and so happy. It was their only happy moment before ... you know, before they were put on a train and .... You are so mean. We hate you! We want to go back home.

NERMINA: Forget the dancers, they weren't real, they just got caught in a snag in time and they turned around so much until they turned to dust. They made me dizzy. You can't live on memories of some God forgotten past. You need food. How much longer are we going to delay our trip in this creepy salt mines with its salt chandeliers? We need food, soup, salad, pudding, quesadilla, dumplings, pumblings, yellow foods, red foods, and a whole bunch of spaghetti. By my calculations we can only last one more day on the reserves we have and if we don't get to Transylvania by tomorrow, we'll all starve to death. Or we'll have to eat our children. And we'll still starve to death because they are too small to satisfy all of us. They are worthless children.

TOMATO and POTATO: Grandma, please, don't eat us, we'll be good children we promise. Tomato keeps making cherry tomatoes for all of you, so you don't starve.

GODDESS: Even I'm starting to get hungry. I thought I was spared that experience, being a fucking Goddess and all. I guess it's the human side of me. We can't eat the children though, it's not civilized. House, you'll have to make one last effort and propel us out of these salt mines back into the salty waters and in the direction of Transylvania.

HOUSE: What am I, fucking Jules Vernes and his thousand leagues under the Sea? Don't you have the boat to propel you?

SINISTRA: The boat is exhausted and is starting to catch water. If we don't get propelled, we'll die both of drowning and of starvation. It's a double whammy death, very unpleasant.

TOMATO: Mom, aren't we already under water? What do you mean the boat is catching water? It's already full of water. We are under water already and we are wearing oxygen masks that our enemy Plastic Bag has provided for us.

MAX: Tomato has a point here. Gee, kids today are so smart! It's all that technology they listen to. It goes to show that the saying "keep your friends close and your enemies even closer" tells the truth. Your enemies are your friends and your friends can go fuck themselves.

ICE CREAM WOMAN: I'm drowning and I'm melting. In fact, I'm melting because I'm drowning. And I'm starving so I'm just going to eat myself. Go fuck yourselves all of you.

GODDESS: Wait, no, my daughter, don't eat yourself. And watch your language. I didn't teach you to cuss like a sailor, you father did.

ICE CREAM WOMAN: We are all a bunch of fucking sorry pathetic drowning sailors, can't you see that? Don't you read the news? We're all under water, the whole fucking world is under water. These are our last minutes on the planet, don't you know that? Let's take a selfie everybody before we all die of drowning, starvation and cannibalism. Fucking smile everybody!

> *Everybody bunches together next to House in a Boat and smiles desperate grotesque smiles. Goddess who is many times bigger than everybody else takes the selfie.*

PLASTIC BAG: Hey don't give up you all. I got news from Transylvania that they are waiting for us and sending rescue submarines to save you all bunch of spineless creeps. Let's see if we can save this planet in one last effort. Don't fucking die, all right? Your families in vampire land are waiting for you, they'll be disappointed if you die or eat each other before you get there.

LOLA MINIATURE WOMAN IN A BOWL (*Diving towards the boat at the bottom of the ocean*): Follow me you troglodytes, I'll show you the way to God in Transylvania and his lot of bandits. I know what you all are after, I heard it through the waves. You want to recuperate the heart of the Goddess, don't you?

ALL: Yes, yes, the heart of the Goddess. She is dying, we are all dying if we don't get to eat something soon. Help us Lola Miniature Woman in a Bowl!

LOLA MINIATURE WOMAN IN A BOWL: You'll have to help me push you up to the surface. You'll never get anywhere crawling at the bottom of the ocean. Your oxygen is thinning out and before you know it, you'll be gasping for air.

TOMATO: Mom, Dad, who is Lola Miniature Woman in a Bowl?

SINISTRA: There is no time for philosophical discussions now honey, we have to just do what Lola says.

MAX: Yes, do what Lola says.

NERMINA: Fucking shut up and do what Lola says.

LOLA MINIATURE WOMAN IN A BOWL(*Towards Tomato*): I'll tell you the story of who I am honey in a second, just let me get this baby moving to the surface and you'll get your answer, I can multitask because I'm well-nourished that's all. And because I'm a girl of course.

> *VOICE: Lola Miniature Woman in a Bowl pushes the boat upwards while the entire crew except for Goddess help push the boat towards the surface of the ocean. Plastic Bag who has been following alongside the boat all along swells himself into a huge protective balloon around the boat to help it move upwards. After strenuous efforts the boat gets to the surface of the ocean and everybody cheers. They all get back inside the boat and start sailing.*

(End of Act III.)

ACT IV- Finding the GODDESS's HEART

All are sailing joyously on the high seas on their way to the Dracula and God the Vampire's castle in Transylvania.

PLASTIC BAG: That was good exercise. I haven't had such a workout since I was Plastic Bag at Walmart a hundred years ago. It goes to show what a recycled Plastic Bag can do. Save the fucking world, that's what!

LOLA MINIATURE WOMAN IN A BOWL: And now let me tell you my story. I am the keeper of tears, the keeper of secrets, of survival tricks, the patron saint of the poor the wretched the hungry the conscientious objectors to Plastic Bag culture. I am the life and the glory, and I do it all in this little China Bowl made in China. They are indestructible. I was sent here by God the father to save you sorry lot of incompetent sailors so you can get to your destination. The whole world depends on you, even God the Father depends on you now. He told me to tell you to hang in there for one more day and try not to starve. He is waiting for you with big fat Transylvanian sausage and pork dumplings.

MAX: I thought God the Father was vegetarian. And I thought he was dead, because I killed him.

LOLA MINIATURE WOMAN IN A BOWL: Well you must not have done a very good job killing him because he is more alive than ever. And voracious. Though he's learned to keep his temper better since he's been in group therapy.

TOMATO: Why is God always so mad, Grandma?

GODDESS: Because he is a fucking psychopath with personality disorder and syphilis, that's why, he stuck his dick in every hole of every creature on earth and now that the whole world is fucked and the number of creatures with holes is highly extinct, he is raving mad. Now you know why.

MAX: Mom I know your heart is missing but really, do you have to rant in this gross way in front of the children? What role model are you?

GODDESS: I'm no role model asshole son, I am the fucking Goddess of the universe, so I talk any way I bloody want.

LOLA MINIATURE WOMAN IN A BOWL: Poor Goddess, she is totally right, let me collect her tears of rage in my bowl to make soup, sweet and sour soup, we can't waste any drop of salty sweet tear water.

>VOICE: LOLA climbs on the Goddess body and collects the tears falling off her chin inside the Bowl which is part of her body.

You know I am stunned at you people. I have been watching you through my binoculars from all the way in Transylvania and marking your progress and I can't believe how much time you waste in your journey talking and blabbering and arguing about everything. What kind of creatures are you? Talk machines? Act more and talk less, that's what the Bible says.

GODDESS: We are itinerant actors, that's who we are. We have to talk and argue because it's part of our roles, and we have to build consensus for all our decisions. We are also community organizers and dispatchers. We dispatch food solutions for the world. We are the last ones left on earth and on water as it is in heaven, all the rest are extinct. We improvise some as we go along of course, but we are who we are, and we are giving one last try to save the world. Isn't that why you are here? To guide us and show us the way to your asshole Vampire boss in Transylvania so we can get back my heart and move on?

POTATO: Yes, we want to see granddaddy the Vampire God and learn to suck blood too.

SINISTRA: We are a bunch of starving fucking artists, that's right. The world is going to be saved by a bunch of starving non-equity actors, and if you say one more word and don't take us to your motherfucking vampire land, I'm going to eat your ass with your China Bowl and all.

LOLA MINIATURE WOMAN IN A BOWL: Not one more word! Follow me!

> VOICE: *The mood is carnivalesque, multicolored, festive. The group of characters looking like a Circus wagon on water travel through more cities under water and on water, mountain chains, the Alps, storms at sea, the Carpathians. They arrive at the foot of a mountain with a dark castle on top, the Vampire God Castle.*

ALL: Wow how beautiful! And it's above water too.

NERMINA: How come this place here has kept its part of land and was not flooded like every other part of earth?

LOLA MINIATURE WOMAN IN A BOWL: Good noticing you all, it's a long story, first things first. Come on now, you've reached the shore, the only shore left on earth, you can anchor your boat to this telephone pole here and step onto Transylvanian land. Come smell the fresh air and eat the polenta. It's called *mamaliga* here, whatever, who cares, it's the same damn tasteless corn mush by whatever name you call it. You know the famous line "a corn mush by any other name it's still a corn mush."

TOMATO and POTATO (*Leaping onto the land in one move*): Mom, Dad, can we drink some blood now? Pleeeaaase, we are hungry and thirsty. We heard that Transylvanian blood has lots of nutrients and it's organic too.

SINISTRA (*Also jumping onto the shore from the boat*): Absolutely not, I already said so: no vampires in my family, no veggie children of mine will ever drink anybody's blood. I'm the only one that can do that, given that I suffer from anemia and postpartum depression. Yikes, but it stinks here. What fresh air are you talking about? It's land and pretty and all with the high mountains and the castle on top, but it stinks like shit on top of vomit on top of rotting corpses. What's going on here, Lola Miniature Woman in a Bowl?

All the rest of the characters, children, Max, Ice Cream Woman, House and Plastic Bag, jump on shore. Only Goddess is still lying along the length of the boat and doesn't want to get off onto the shore.

MAX: Come on Mom, why don't you come join us onshore, we came all the way here for you and your heart, so you can save humanity and bring back food and earth. It's true it stinks here like a thousand rotting horses, but once you get used to it it's not too bad.

GODDESS: No, it's all right, you all go ahead without me. I'm rather tired from the months of traveling on and under water. I'm afraid if we let go of the boat, it will go away and we'll be stranded here forever. We need the boat, whatever the outcome of this visit here will be.

MAX: All right, whatever, have it your way mom, you always have your way.

VOICE: Deafening roars are heard as if coming from a large beast, a bear or a roar producing machine turned to its highest volume. Following the roar, a monstrous enormous creature covered in blood, excrement, rags, rotting food, gasoline, plastic bags, credit cards, human and animal hair and one hundred-dollar bills makes its appearance. It is God.

ALL: Oh my God!

GOD (*He is sitting in a throne made of plastic bottles and tin cans and talks in a high-pitched voice that contrasts with the roaring heard earlier and his gruesome appearance.*): Thank you, thank you, I *am* your God, make yourselves at home, come over here in the back of the castle it's cooler, shadier.

ALL (*Whispering to one another in horror. Lines are to be divided among all the characters*):

What are we going to do?

God is one huge pile of moving shit.

How are we going to pass by him and get the heart from the castle?

Plus, even if we can trick him, we'll all die from the stench before we reach the Goddess heart. I say we get back in the boat and sail away.

Life on water isn't so bad, and it smells better.

Plus, Goddess seems to be getting by just fine without a heart, just with her brain and a hundred vaginas.

GODDESS: No way, no how, you cowardly good for nothing creeps! I heard what you said, my vaginas have perfect hearing. You get off your bony stupid asses, and go kill this pile of excrement God and get my heart from the box in the castle or you'll all die of painful starvation and drowning. I've had it with you crowd of untalented actors.

MAX: All right mom, we'll do it. I wish I had killed him better the last time, I didn't realize God was so resilient.

LOLA MINIATURE WOMAN IN A BOWL: That's because you don't know your holy books, that's why. Do a better job this time and cut off all his channels of resurrection, that's what you need to do. It's what the Hindus do when they kill their God. You need to expand your culture a bit more, to the east and the south and the Pacific Midwest what the fuck!

GOD: Just look at that, what a surprise, Princess Mitzi and her pathetic crowd of miscreants.

GODDESS: You call me Mitzi one more time and I'll expose your big dark secret, you piece of worthless smoldering shit.

GOD: Oooh, I love it when she talks dirty. Don't you worry pussycat I have secrets to reveal too about you and your hundred no-brain vaginas.

MAX: Mom, Dad please stop arguing, there is no time for this crap, we don't have much time don't you get that, this is our last chance to save the world and put some food in our stomachs before we all die. And if we die, you die and this whole pile of shit you call country God and family goes to fucking hell. All food is almost extinct, the waters keep rising, soon we'll all be food for sharks and then even the sharks will die after they have eaten us, and it will all be dark and empty and silent. Only a big hole filled with water is all that will be left.

GOD: You must take after your mother with your doomsday talk and wobbly walk. So how do you plan to save the world, beloved son and ex-wife?

ALL (*Whispering to each other so God doesn't hear them. Lines should be divided among all actors*): Should we tell him he has to return the Goddess heart?

No, he will never give it to us, that's what's sustaining him, the juices from the Goddess heart, otherwise he would be a dried-up piece of excrement dead at the bottom of the ocean.

I say we come clean and tell him what we came here for, he sounds like he wants to save the world too.

No he doesn't, he wants to just save himself and a few of his best whores and let the bit of the world that is left go to the bottom of the ocean like the Eiffel Tower and the Tower of Pisa and the needle in the haystack.

Somebody make a decision, establish a consensus, we don't have much time left!

Let's vote.

Fuck voting, it's rigged!

MAX: Mom, it's your heart, you decide how you want to go about this whole thing. I already killed dad once and he's come back with a vengeance and orange hair. Now it's your turn to destroy the mother fucker. Use your womanly guile.

GODDESS (*After a few seconds of intense thinking, writhing, crying*): Yes, I'll go the old-fashioned way, I'll use my "womanly guile" like my son put it so well. I never failed giving him a hard-on.

MAX and ICE CREAM WOMAN: Mom, please, we don't want to hear about your sex life with dad, it's gross. Plus, it's so backwards and old fashioned, but if it's the last resort, just do what you have to do, and we'll support you.

GODDESS: I never liked it, he was so brutish and always stunk like shit. I cheated on him with every girl and boy I could get my hands on or stick in my vaginas. Sometimes two or three at a time, all consensual though, ha, ha, ha!

> *She laughs hysterically and gets out of the boat. She is huge standing up, many times as big as everybody else.*

Hey Bruce! Nice to see you, how have you been my love, still fucking the same old whores? It's been lonely without you!

> *Aside towards the other characters.*

Vomit on him a million times.

POTATO and TOMATO: What? God's real name is Bruce? That's the funniest thing I ever heard. I thought his real name is Pinocchio, or Dracula, one of the two or both.

GOD: Oh, I love it when you call me Bruce, that's how we made Max, remember, you called me Bruce, one thing led to another and before you knew it, your belly was as big as the Himalayas. Listen, did you bring me some pizza?

GODDESS: Pizza is extinct, Bruce! Hot dogs are extinct, apple pie is extinct. Plastic Bag rules, it's a jungle out there, we survived on scraps and almost ate our children and grandchildren on the journey here.

Aren't you going to ask us to stay for dinner? I heard you have some polenta.

GOD: Where did you hear that?

GODDESS: Everybody knows, the word moves fast under water.

GOD: Well since you put it this way, I'll have the minion vampires and whores prepare you the best Transylvanian *mamaliga* you've ever eaten. Nobody makes better polenta *mamaliga* than a good whore, ha, ha, I could die of laughter. We had polenta on our first date in Rome, in the Coliseum, remember my beauty? You only had one plump vagina then, that's all, oh the good old times.

> *VOICE: House in a Boat comes out of the boat onto land shaking, rattling and roaring, moving threateningly towards GOD, she spews out sentences algae red fishes mud as in the first incoherent soliloquy, a purging of the collective subconscious.*

HOUSE IN A BOAT: God is an impostor don't listen to him don't eat his food don't drink his water it's infested by his sex trafficking in women and vampires, God is a slave owner and a sex trafficker and a Dracula impersonator vampires aren't so bad they can be good for your health actually they can cleanse your blood of all the plastic you've eaten and the gasoline you've drunk out of a sense of moral obligation because you wanted to believe in God almighty the son and the spirit and the holy crap, get back in line you all you need a House with food and a king size bed you all forgot where you came from where you come from where you are going to come from you all forgot your House of origin under water underground in addition God is an American CEO, he fucked you all, now you need to repent start over go bipartisan with Plastic Bag at the head of your movement revolution to capture the heart of the Goddess Violeta the life and the glory there will never be another planet like the earth with funnel cake and cotton candy and all the cucurbits and night shade vegetables in the middle of a large field with cows and homemade bread and the whole shebang shebang God never existed he was just an American bandito who wanted your food your women your minds your minds most of all it's the conspiracy of all conspiracies, this is all a sham a pretend country government alleluia who art in heaven as it is on earth and in your mother's ass forever and ever he usurped the Goddess from her primordial throne of chocolate and cocoa butter when all the races lived in peace without profiling anybody the secret is in the Goddess heart the heart the heart.

> *Everybody is stunned and mesmerized even God who stands frozen in an obscene position. Sinistra and Nermina take advantage of the distraction and immobilize God in his obscene position. House continues to shake and rattle and move around God trying to keep him from moving in any direction.*

GODDESS: Good job girls, keep God from taking even one step, with every step he takes he destroys the little that is left of the world, with every breath he breathes he poisons the air, with every word he utters he darkens the skies.

LOLA MINIATURE WOMAN IN A BOWL: God is a Christian fundamentalist atheist creep, he doesn't even believe in his own motherfucking self.

ALL: Oooh, God is an atheist?

MAX: I knew it, I always knew there was something fishy about dad! What do we do now? He is the only one who knows where the Goddess heart is hidden. We can't kill him yet until he tells us the secret place. Maybe just torture him a bit? For example, water board him a little? He's always been scared of water.

NERMINA: We don't torture our enemies; torture doesn't work and is messy. We are the holy family; we believe in love!

SINISTRA: Fuck love, mom, it never works, how has love worked for you so far? Look at the apocalypse we are all in!

POTATO and TOMATO: Maybe granddaddy is just hungry, don't torture him mama! You are a mean bitch of a mommy. We love our granddaddy ugly and smelly as he is.

ICE CREAM WOMAN: The kids have a point, the children these days are so good with technology. Maybe they can twitter God a secret message, he likes that, and make him reveal the hiding place of the Goddess heart. Maybe he can find his true self in a tweet shit, his Pinocchio self and fuck himself with his own nose in his own ass.

PLASTIC BAG: You are such an inspiration for us all, Ice Cream Woman, and a poet too. If I weren't in such a hurry, I'd lick your brains out. Follow me everybody, I just got a tweet from Dracula, he said "hashtag secret passage room inside room spiral staircase big opening basement top of the mountain Goddess heart, lots of pussycats hashtag God likes crack cocaine." It's pretty clear isn't it? Here I've got the powder for God's overdose, and then we can proceed. Dracula was God's lover for a while and got terribly hurt when GOD cheated on him with one of the eunuchs vampire boys and promised to destroy him.

ALL: God is an American CEO atheist crack cocaine addict child molester?

MAX: Suddenly God doesn't sound so bad, I'm starting to feel sorry for dad, maybe all he needed was a good mental health program, a good Mafia therapist. He is too fucked up and too dumb to be evil.

GODDESS: Don't do it son, don't let your pity get the best of you, that's how he got to me too, every time. Let's follow Plastic Bag, he knows better, he's been around and will be around forever, Plastic Bag never dies.

> *Plastic Bag gives God his portion of drugs while Sinistra and Nermina immobilize him. God becomes almost unconscious.*

PLASTIC BAG: Like hell he doesn't, ask Ms. Polymeric apocalypse here about that! All right, I've gotten him drugged up enough, he won't know what's going on. And by the time he comes to, we'll be in the possession of the heart. Come on, we don't have much time!

POTATO: Mr. Plastic Bag are you a non-equity actor like my mom and dad too?

TOMATO: Yes, Mr. Plastic Bag, do you have a penis or a vagina?

PLASTIC BAG: I swear I'm gonna extinct these kids when all this madness is over. Shut the fuck up and do what you're told, or you'll be Potato Tomato stew before you can say fart.

> VOICE: The whole group follows Plastic Bag through tortuous paths of the Dracula castle, spiraling stairs, caves, secret passages, a ball room, a torture room, a room inside a room that opens into a green meadow with flowers of all colors, foods of all colors and flavors and three boxes on top of a golden table. Under a circus like tent at the edges of the meadow is an exhibit of cats from all over the world, of all breeds, sitting quietly in cages. Vivian Big Woman in a Tree presides over the stunningly beautiful and pristine nature, over the food, the three boxes, and the cats exhibit, like a judge. Dracula is sitting next to her in a delicate rocking chair dressed in a pink tutu. He is pretty, small, and feminine and he is crying.

VIVIAN BIG WOMAN IN A TREE: Welcome to Transylvania land of the flour and home of the bread! Make yourself at home, please, fe fi fom I smell blood of a Transylvania man. One of you is from around here, I sense it, one of them returning refugees, your acting career didn't work out so well out there, did it? In any case, no time to waste on empty talk. You've come just in time to save the world and your own sorry wet asses from definitive and eternal starvation. You have to pass three tests.

DRACULA: Bambino lambino rumple stumble gloo gloo girgle girgle ga ga gugu. I hate God.

GODDESS: You and me both!

DRACULA: GOD is peepee and caca!

GODDESS: Well put Dracula, you are such a smart boy. And you've grown a lot since I last saw you in your last production.

DRACULA: Mama, caca, peepee, poopoo, squamous sperm, God profiled me when I was minding my business impaling the ants on a hill and some bad Turks and stunted my intellectual growth and put me in a box of dried up skeletons and scared me to death until I died. And then God stole my secret and sold it to Texas and racially profiled me and made a big stereotype about me that makes the Transylvanian people look bad in the world of art and then he broke my heart with his stupid tiny penis. God is an ugly piece of shit. I don't even like blood, I'm allergic to blood, I only like macadamia nuts and gingerbread.

VIVIAN BIG WOMAN IN A TREE: You'll have to forgive him, he has become dyslexic and suffers from PTSD and postpartum depression after the birth of his newest child, Dracula junior. Go play with your baby son and with your kitty cats Dracula honey, this is too stressful for you, these people are ruthless and hungry, they might want to eat you. Go, go, I'll call you when they are all gone. Then we can play penis and vagina again.

DRACULA: Yay! I love Vivian Big Woman in a Tree. She is the best Mother Nature in the world, only she understands who I really am. And I am bing bang bong!

VIVIAN BIG WOMAN IN A TREE: Don't mind him, he's been through a lot lately, he gave all his blood to God who is the real Vampire. So, are you ready for your test?

TOMATO: Mom, can Potato and I take the tests? Our brains are smarter, and we got a good education in intrauterine school.

HOUSE (*Crying softly and tenderly, emotionally*): If you fail the tests I will have to eat you two, you were conceived and born inside me and you will have to go back inside me, it's how it works, once a House always a House and what goes around comes around. I gave you a good education you have to make me proud on the eve of destruction it's all we've got it's who we are make Transylvania great again die for your country eat shit and die.

VIVIAN BIG WOMAN IN A TREE: There you go! House said it better than I could have ever said it. Here are your three tests: the Goddess heart is divided in three, one piece is in one of the boxes, one piece inside one of the cats, one piece inside the one of you who is the returning refugee and has been carrying the Goddess heart all along all over the fucking world and the rotting seas. Now it's the time of return and remembrance. You have three minutes to find the heart pieces. Good luck, get ready, set, fucking go!

> *Great commotion among the characters, they consult with one another frenetically, whisper, scream, argue. Nermina silences them all.*

NERMINA (*Trance-like*): I remember my childhood in a Transylvanian plum tree with an ugly hairless cat that I adored and a pretty fluffy cat that I hated and eating plums in a sour cherry tree with quinces all night long in the summer and winter and all year round we grew our own crops and raised our own Houses and Dracula was our cute uncle who wouldn't hurt a fly, we played hide and seek, but one day a bad dictator came and Dracula impaled one of the ants in the ant hill and that's when I knew everybody was becoming an Impaler so I swam across the Atlantic Ocean and got to Cleveland Ohio on a nasty day of mass shootings and got a PhD in feline philology the hairless ugly cat followed me everywhere she was a loyal cat never judge a cat by its hair, the American dream took a big dump in the Ohio river and there I met my future husband who was a handsome Maltese falcon man with mustache and the works really he turned out to be a child molesting creep so I killed him in a boating accident and dumped him in the Ohio river and from that love story was born my one and only daughter Sinistra. I raised her in a pretty House on the prairie until a tornado came and before we knew it everything was under water and all the food was gone that's when I knew I had to get inside a boat with House and travel the world and find the hairless cat called Mitzi who ate one third of the Goddess heart because one day when she was high on drugs she was hungry and took the third of the heart for a mouse and ate it but then it felt so good having part of the Goddess heart inside her that she didn't want to give it back, but Dracula applied the Heimlich maneuver and made her spit it out but she was stubborn and ate it right back and said I'll keep the third of the heart swallowed until queen Nermina comes back and lots of other adventures on the sea and under the sea. I had to feed my starving daughter, she had developed eating disorders and became a cannibal daughter, she gave birth to bulbous children and then everybody came on board and helped out and here we all are, of the three boxes, one glittering gold, one diamond and sapphires, one worm eaten wood, I choose the worn out ugly wooden box eaten by worms. Don't judge a box by its cover and here you have it the ugly box was hiding the first third of the Goddess heart who would have thought it. And here is the second third of the Goddess heart I swallowed and took with me when I immigrated so I don't die of longing, it saved my life and the lives of my family and here it is I give it back to the land of the flour and home of the bread where vampires are profiled by the American police and Dracula is a delicate pretty homeless man who wouldn't hurt a fly only impale an ant, nothing is perfect but at least we have land and the people are kind.

She gags out a third of the heart.

VIVIAN BIG WOMAN IN A TREE: Wow fantastic! You passed the test, so you are the Transylvanian bitch who left us to fend for ourselves, good for you, look at you how accomplished you have become sailing the waters of the apocalypse. And look at that, you saved all the sex slaves he kept, see all the cats are turning back into the beautiful maidens they once were and that he stole from each country he visited. The sphinx hairless one was Angela Merkel, good guess, he hated her more than any of them. Good for you that you guessed she had the last third of the Goddess heart, she's the best nasty woman ever!

GOD (*Appearing in a crazed state roaring and wearing a KKK cape and hood.*) Don't give her the heart or I'll impale you all like you've never been impaled before then you'll know who is boss.

MAX: Dad, I've had it with you and your psycho childish hateful no good rapist mafia CEO crap, I renounce you and your entire race, I renege you and unfather and defather you from me. I reborn myself again from mama's hundred vaginas, I'm done with you, here eat this and die. You and your bunch of creepy penis friends failed us all, failed us all, fucking failed and furfunkled us into itchy nothingness, nothing is real, you are not even wearing brains only a red orange wig where did you get your sense of style anyways you are not even wearing a liver and half a brain you raped mama a million times and killed all her children, me and Ice Cream are the only survivors, surviva, survivo, survivamos as our ancestors the Romans once said.

PLASTIC BAG: Yes GOD, I've waited for this moment my whole entire life, eat this and die, eat my skin, eat my dick and my cunt and my polymerous substance. I suicide bomb myself so the world can live. Long live suicide bomb of God by Plastic Bag. Die asshole!

GOD(*Writhing in pain*):Aaaaaah, I should have known better you communist, you bad immigrant all women are bad and cunts whoever invented them I fucked my daughter a million times too just so you know I fed you at my breast and raised you like my own son, I should have killed you and your entire family of buttfucking Mexican terrorists!

> *VOICE: God and Plastic Bag explode in a suicide bomb that bursts into myriads of colors and then dissipates into nothingness. Cheerful circus music covers the explosion sounds.*

POTATO and TOMATO: Here grandma Goddess the three pieces of heart, can we put them back in your body? They are so pretty and plump, just like cherry tomatoes.

SINISTRA: Good job kids, I'm so proud of you, good sharing and good listening!

POTATO and TOMATO (*Struggling to put the heart pieces inside Goddess*): Gee grandma, your vaginas stink, you have yeast infections.

GODDESS: I know, I'm itching like mad, this is what living without a heart on the sea in the vicinity of Plastic Bag will do to you. Good thing I've got my brains, they saved my butt.

TOMATO and POTATO: Grandma you are funny, we love you! We miss Plastic Bag though, he was a hero, he was funny too, he was a hermaphrodite, he had both a penis and a vagina and he killed granddaddy in a magnificent nonteroristic way hooray for mercy killing, we are good children we love you grandma.

HOUSE: Look at that! The earth is coming back! What did I tell you, the waters are withdrawing look at all the foods out there, I can have squash and marmalade again, pizza with ketchup, onions and heirloom parsnips, green curry and minestrone, corn mush à la carte and yuca with mocha with cabbage pie, I can feed all my children, I'll never be hungry again Tara, Tara!

ICE CREAM WOMAN: What do I see, what do I see, an ice cream tree all the flavors pistachio and farfadelle al forno, what's your topping what's yours up yours where are you from, what's your accent who did your mother fuck when she was a duck?

TOMATO: What did I tell you? Here are my brothers and sisters the big tomatoes on the vines, we are all going to fuck each other and make trillions of others like us in our image of ripeness incest works in the veggie kingdom, just relax it's ok.

POTATO: Mama, I like your vagina but you also have brains and are a festive refugee from the blood of Dracula and the impaled Turkish people I want my country back I miss you mama, ok goodbye I'll marry Tomato ok goodbye again.

SINISTRA: The rainbow will always feed us its berry mousse, somewhere over the rainbow lays a big pile of shit in the country where we were Black Polish people but now we made it all better and saved the sharks didn't kill them and saved the cats didn't kill them just dehearted one, my mama's favorite ugly sphinx hairless one but we needed to do that sometimes a sacrifice is all you've got amen! Look at the plums in the trees at the mulberry wine just look at that as someone once said that the cactus flower doesn't live in the desert it lives in the desert in the oasis of aloe Vera sprinkled with vampire blood all good, bamba la bamba let's dance Max my love look how you've grown you are no longer a baby you are my forever dancer now we can go with the dance people in their snagged moment in time the waltzes of salt crystal chandeliers a moment the moment is always a ripe banana, fuck me I was hungry like a million extinct she wolves!

MAX: Sinistra if I had only known life at sea was so hard I would have been a girl, a daughter of Goddess without God, I'm sorry I got it all wrong once in a lifetime comes a time when you renege your father and by any other name it's still a fucking armadillo all life that once existed and your pussy so sweet and sour I could eat it all day, will you marry me and make Potato and Tomato children to ensure the resurrection of the species, fuck the species, we missed all our chances there is a full and total eclipse of the moon, mama will you ever forgive me, I'll take care of you from now on, Dad will never come back this time I killed him good.

GODDESS(*Speaking directly to audience*): Ladies and gentlemen the moral of this story is: you can't keep a good girl hungry and you can't steal her heart, or she'll shred you to pieces and send you to sea for a thousand years and then eat you. And one more thing, very important, make your own food, be your own food, share your own food, be your own earth. Earth is food. And love your mothers, don't eat your mothers, alright, they made you! We hope you liked our story of the end and the beginning of the world, it's a true story. The End.

> *VOICE: Sea and land are parted by Goddess, the waters withdraw, and golden beaches appear at the bottom of the Carpathian Mountains covered in dark pine forests, meadows with wildflowers, fruit orchards, vegetable gardens, a bountiful and glorious nature.*
>
> *At the top of the mountain the Dracula castle rises magnificently in white stone and red tile roofs. The group of characters/actors led by Goddess are waltzing on the path*

towards the castle in a joyous mood. The sun is setting on the mountains and on the sea waters that glow in the twilight.

THE END

(Blackout)

Crossings.

A Play of Immigrant Voices

This play is dedicated to those who cross borders every day, to those who survive and persist, to those who have perished and continue to perish in their strenuous crossings.

In Homage to the play *Manual for a Desperate Crossing* by Maria Irene Fornes

Praise for *Crossings*:

Crossings is a rare play. While it is based on research and testimony from people who made the crossings the play depicts, Radulescu invests the play with her own sense of composition, rhythm and structure that lends a greater urgency than what you'd find with a typical documentary. In a time when it is hard to decipher the real from the fake news, *Crossings* offers its audiences a rare experience to taste the truth of what is happening today at our borders.

Radulescu has a strong sense of the visual and how to bring many different voices into a coherent ensemble. The bilingual aspects of the play provide English-speaking audiences a chance to realize what it's like to be a stranger in a strange land. *Crossings* not only educates its audiences about how people from México and Central America got here, it opens our hearts.

> *Emma Godman-Sherman*, Award winning playwright, author of *Abraham's Daughters*, founder and resident dramaturg of 29th Street Playwriting Collective.

<u>Development History</u>:

Crossings was developed in the 29th Street Playwriting Collective workshop in the fall of 2019 with professional New York based actors. The last Tableau was presented at the Goddard Riverside Center as a staged reading on November 20th, 2019.

Crossings was also part of the WHAM festival at the Riverside Center on March 14th and was scheduled for presentation in its entirety but the production was cancelled due to the Corona virus pandemic.

<u>Notes on Play Creation</u>

The present work has emerged from interviews with immigrants and refugees from México, Guatemala and Honduras. All names have been changed to protect their identities. Some of the stories are as recent as several months, others date from the early or late 2000s. All the people interviewed live in Virginia, work strenuous jobs, take care of their families here in the United States as well as help their families back in their native countries.

This play must be produced with great simplicity yet with rhythm, visual beauty and imagery. It should be both musical, stylized and raw, combining the actors' voices and stage movements with projections of deserts, mountains, rivers, real detention centers at the border. It must be beautiful and terrifying all at the same time.

For the sake of authenticity many of the lines of the refugee characters and the Coyotes are a combination of Spanish and English. The actors playing the refuge characters and the Coyotes must be bilingual or at least have some basic ability to speak/pronounce Spanish.

CHARACTERS (In order of speaking parts):

YSABEL – Mexican woman in her mid to late forties, kind, hard-working, carries a perpetual sadness in her eyes. She also acts as translator for the other characters

MATEO – Mexican man in his forties, timid, soft spoken, sweet

CANDELA – Mexican woman in her early thirties, outspoken, proud

MERCEDES – Honduran woman in her late forties, pious, strong

PEDRA – Honduran woman in her late thirties, positive, moody

ANITA – Guatemalan woman in her late twenties, upbeat, dynamic

COYOTE – Mexican man in his forties, strong, harsh, no-nonsense

IMMIGRATION OFFICER – American man in his thirties, cocky, aggressive, with a Texan accent

CHORUS – The immigrant characters form a chorus in key moments which, like in Greek tragedy, accentuates the mood or the emotional intensity of the stories, clarifies them or reacts to them and offers moral support. Depending on who is telling their story at any given moment, CHORUS is formed in an ad-hoc manner by the other characters who are listening. The actors are also spectators. They are telling their own stories, reliving or re-enacting them but also becoming characters in each other's stories.

SETTING

An empty stage with only a suggestion of a wire fence behind which the characters move and speak, separated from the audience. Projections of the desert, of rivers, forests or mountains as backdrops to the different stories, rotating throughout the play. Only in the middle of the last Tableau the wire fence disappears, and the empty stage suggests a safe space, a yard behind YSABEL's house in Virginia.

TIME

The present and mid to late -2010s in flashbacks. Memory and the present time are continuously intertwined. The scenes in the past are acted out as dreamscapes, where everything shifts in the past and all actors are acting out the respective episode in one of the characters' story.

TABLEAU I

Why Did you Leave Your Country?

¿Por qué dejaste tu país?

Actors who play immigrants arrive from both sides of the stage, some walking slowly and fearfully, some running or crawling. All carry small bags or suitcases. First lines are staggered in whispers, which become louder until they turn to screams then they become rhythmical, like a song. It all stops abruptly.

CHORUS:

Sonora

Tijuana

El desierto

Sonora

El desierto de Sonora

Río Bravo

The river

Los potreros

Las montañas

El río

La lancha

The boat

The desert

The river

Tijuana

The desert

The river

The mountains

Sonora

La lancha

YSABEL (*Looking around suspiciously*): Why did you leave your country?

CHORUS (*They are all getting up slowly, checking around them*): ¿Qué, ¿qué dice?

YSABEL: ¿Por qué dejaste tu país?

CHORUS: Aaaahhh!

MATEO: Estaba yo pasando una situación, una situación difícil de ...

YSABEL (*Speaking directly to the audience like an interpreter*): He was going through a situation, through a difficult situation of ...

CHORUS: ¿Qué situación? ¿qué situación? ¿Una situación difícil de qué?

MATEO: Una situación de drogas ... y económicamente era muy, muy difícil ... no tenía nada que comer, mis hijos casi se morían de hambre, y las bandas ...

YSABEL (*Same as before, speaking to the audience*): A situation of drugs ... and economically, it was very, very difficult ... his children were starving ... and the gangs ...

MATEO: Mi abuelo me dijo ...

CHORUS: Que, ¿qué te dijo tu abuelo?

YSABEL: What did your grandfather tell you?

MATEO: Me dijo que viniera a los Estados Unidos.

YSABEL (*Same as before, to the audience like an interpreter*): His grandfather told him to come to the United States. To get away from the gangs ...

CANDELA: My brother was here ... I had to leave, the narcos ... Yo no sabía que estaba embarazada ...

YSABEL: Oh, you didn't know you were pregnant when you left, how old were you?

CANDELA: I was eighteen, I was pregnant, I didn't know it ... I wanted to be with my brother ... he was here en los Estados Unidos. I was only three months pregnant and didn't know it.

MERCEDES: La razón ... estaba pasando un momento muy difícil, el Señor me abrió una puerta. Yo trabajaba mucho, mi Mamá estaba muy enferma, trabajaba 16 horas al día, mi esposo abusaba de mí ... eran pandillas ...

YSABEL: She was going through a difficult moment ... but God opened a door for her... She was working sixteen hours a day to help her family, her mother was very sick, her husband was abusing her ... There were gangs ...

MERCEDES: Hay bandas, muchas bandas, de los Maras ...

YSABEL: There are gangs, many gangs, the maras ...!

CHORUS: Oohh, las maras, las maras, malditas maras, ¡te van a matar!

YSABEL: The maras kill you, they are going to kill you with no pity, your children, your entire family, they will kill you.

PEDRA: Yo salí del país para poder ayudar a mis hermanos. Yo salí el 12 de febrero. Hacía mucho frío y decidí irme porque era mi cumpleaños. ¡No había trabajo! ¡Ningún trabajo! No quería más vivir así.

YSABEL: She left her country to help her brothers. There was no work. None. No work at all. She left the 12th of February, on her birthday, she couldn't stand the difficulties anymore and wanted to help her brothers.

CHORUS: ¿Y las maras? ¿Las bandas?

YSABEL and PEDRA: Yes, yes, the maras, of course, the gangs, always! ¡Siempre las Maras! ¡Te amenazan que te van a matar y matar a toda la familia ... they threaten they will kill you and your whole family!

MERCEDES: Estaba pasando un momento difícil.

YSABEL: She was going through a difficult moment. Working mother, her husband was abusing her! And the gangs!

ANITA: El motivo ... que salí de mi país fue por la falta del empleo, estaba sola, llego un momento difícil donde mi vida corría peligro ... las pandillas, ¡las maras! Tiene que haber algo muy fuerte para tomar esa decisión.

YSABEL: You had no job, you were alone, your life was in danger ... there were gangs, the maras! Yes, there must be a very strong reason to take this decision, to leave everything!

ANITA: Este fue el motivo – mi hermano was asked to be part of a gang, or they would kill him, the maras, fue la razón principal.

CHORUS (*Chant like*): Las Maras, las Maras, malditas Maras, lo van a matar, ¡te van a matar!

> *The next lines are overlapping, as actors cross the stage in a frenzy, putting things in their bags, suitcases, packing for the escape. The lines are shared among the characters.*

El señor me abrió una puerta,

estaba pasando un momento difícil, eran las Maras ...

God opened a door, it was hard, there were gangs ...

My life was in danger ...

Una situación de drogas ...

¡Ningún trabajo, yo salí el 12 febrero! ¡Quería ayudar a mi familia!

Yo no sabía que estaba embarazada

She was pregnant but didn't know it ...

La maleta ... tres mudas ... la maletita, para el camino ...

The suitcase ... three changes of clothes, the little suitcase for the road ...

CHORUS: La maleta, la maletita, tres mudas, agua, agua, agua, ¡para el camino! The suitcase, three changes of clothes, water, water, water, for the road! Take water for the road, take the suitcase for the difficult road, take a picture of your family. Water, suitcase, picture!

End of TABLEAU I

(Blackout)

TABLEAU II

How Did you Cross the Border?

¿Cómo cruzaste la frontera?

All actors playing immigrant characters come on to the stage running from different directions, some from both sides of the stage, some from the audience, holding their luggage, looking around them with suspicion and fear. Sounds of voices, coyotes howling, muffled cries, like the beginning of ACT I, only more intensified.

CHORUS (*The following lines are to be said almost in a chant like manner, rhythmically, becoming louder and more accelerated*):

En autobús

Caminando

On the bus,

Walking

En camión

In a truck

Cruzamos el río

Cruzamos el desierto

Cruzamos los potreros

We crossed the river

We crossed the desert

We crossed the mountains

Cruzamos caminando la frontera de Guatemala

Cruzamos caminando la frontera de México

Cruzamos caminando la frontera de los Estados Unidos

We walked across the border with Guatemala

We walked across the border with México

We walked across the border with the United States

Estaba inmigración

Estaba inmigración

Estaba inmigración

Inmigración, inmigración, inmigración ...

YSABEL: ¿Dime, ¿Cómo cruzaste ¿Cómo saliste? ¿Cómo te viniste? How did you cross, how did you leave, how did you come? Tell me!

PEDRA: Yo salí el 12 de febrero ...

YSABEL (*All the following lines are to be delivered quickly, breathlessly. At times Ysabel translates using the first person, other times the third person, there is no rule*): I left the 12th of February ...

PEDRA: Cruce caminando la frontera de Guatemala, me tomo seis días, pues la frontera de México, pero no pude caminar, estaba inmigración, nadé por el río para cruzar.

YSABEL: Wow, she crossed the border with Guatemala, it took her six days, then the frontier with México. They couldn't walk across, there was immigration, they swam across the river ...

CHORUS: (*Chant like, with a rhythmic beat*): Ella cruzo the border with Guatemala, le tomo six days, la frontera de México, inmigración, el rio, the river, immigration ...

MATEO: Fue algo pesado, it was difficult ... el viaje en autobús - twenty-six hours on the bus ... We met the coyote at the border, caminamos 6 horas en la noche sin saber a dónde llegaríamos.

YSABEL: They walked six hours at night without knowing where they were going.

CANDELA: Caminamos por el desierto de Sonora ... caminamos el desierto, todo fue a pie ... sin río.

YSABEL: We walked across the Sonora desert ... there was no river, only desert.

MATEO: No tenía nada más que la ropa que llevábamos de México. Muchas veces te espinabas la cara, no podías usar ninguna lampara ...

YSABEL: We only had the clothes we wore from México, many times you scratched your face, you couldn't use any flashlight ...

CANDELA: The weight, the heat ... Yo traje una maletita con pastillas, una botella de agua, teníamos miedo nosotros...

YSABEL: El pesar, el calor ... I carried a little suitcase with pills, a bottle of water. We were scared ...

CHORUS: Una maleta, una maletita, pastillas, agua, cómo nosotros. Like us, the suitcase, the little suitcase, pills, water, we were scared! We followed the coyotes; they take your money but know the roads.

MERCEDES: El frío, el calor ... Caminamos, y caminamos más y más, y más ...

CHORUS: Y más, y más, y más, more and more and more walking ..., días, semanas, caminando, days and weeks walking and walking and walking.

> *They are walking in place and in sync with each other, almost like a ballet.*

MERCEDES: Dormimos en el suelo, en los potreros, había niños pequeños de 5 años, y de 8 años el mayor, de la edad de más chiquitos ...

YSABEL: You slept on the ground, in the ...? ¿Qué significa potreros?

MERCEDES: Potreros – cómo montañas ...

YSABEL: Aahh, las montañas, you slept in the mountains for days ... There were small children, as young as five, eight years old ...?

MERCEDES: Había personas ... no quiero decir, no se podía pasar, entonces se detenía el grupo ... El señor vigilaba por nosotros ...

YSABEL: Ooohh, there were people ... She doesn't want to say, they couldn't pass, there were people holding up the group ... The Lord was watching over them.

MERCEDES: Nos bañamos en el río. ¡Vivimos en los potreros 2 meses, sin nada.

YSABEL: Oh yes, you bathed in the river ... they bathed in the river, they lived in the mountains for a month and two weeks, without anything! Waiting, and waiting for the right moment.

CHORUS: Nos bañamos en el rio ... We bathed in the river .... Nos bañamos en el rio ... Rio Bravo, Rio Grande, la lancha ..., the boat, river, river, river. Waiting, esperando, waiting, esperando, two months!

YSABEL: Yo estoy interesada en eso ... Su historia me parece muy interesante ... Pero cuando salí de su país, ¿usted trajo una maleta, que trajo?

> *Turning towards the audience and translating her own words in a conspiratorial manner. Here she becomes almost professorial trying to understand and interpret Mercedes's story for the audience.*

I am particularly interested in this ... I find her story very interesting ... Don't you? I am wondering, when she left her country, did she carry a suitcase, what did she carry, what?

MERCEDES: Traje una mochila, mi ropa interior ... Y tres mudas.

YSABEL: Ooh, you were carrying a backpack, underwear and three outfits. Solamente tres mudados. Only three changes of clothes.

CHORUS (*In rhythm, chant like, while walking across the stage with backpacks and suitcases*): Una maleta y tres mudas, una maleta y tres mudas, una mochila y tres mudas ...

YSABEL: Yes, a suitcase, three outfits, a suitcase, three outfits ...

CHORUS: A suitcase and three outfits ... that's all! Just like us. ¡Cómo todos nosotros!

PEDRA: Y una botella de agua.

CANDELA: Si, una botella de agua, cruzamos el desierto ...

CHORUS: A bottle of water for the desert, that's all. In the desert, we crossed the desert with solamente una botella de agua, ¡wow! Only a bottle of water, wow!

MERCEDES: Con Inmigración en la frontera no podía pasar el río. Yo estuve un mes 15 días en la frontera.

YSABEL: She couldn't cross because of immigration. She stayed one month and fifteen days at the border with México.

MERCEDES: Y entonces pasamos en lancha, el rio. Pasamos en la madrugada, a las dos de la mañana, cuidadosamente, silenciosamente ...

YSABEL: Then we crossed the river in a boat. We crossed early in the morning, at 2 in the morning, carefully, silently ...

MERCEDES: Y yo vigilaba la lancha, El Señor vigilaba por nosotros, gracias a Dios, podemos pasar a esta hora ... Ahí volvimos y caminamos mucho, caminamos más y más ... Nos tomó dos meses por todo para llegar ...

YSABEL: I was praying in the boat, God was watching over us, thank God, we could pass at that hour ... There we turned around ... and walked again, we walked a lot, we walked and walked ... it took us two months in all to arrive.

MERCEDES: ¡Dos meses para cruzar, dos meses para llegar! Two months to cross, two months to arrive ...

CHORUS: Two months to cross, two months to arrive ... a lot of time to arrive... ¡Mucho tiempo para cruzar, mucho tiempo para llegar!

ANITA: Yo salí de Honduras, llegó en 3 días a Guatemala, después salí a México tomando autobús. I left Honduras and I got to Guatemala in 3 days, I left for México in a bus. I only came with my brother who was 12. La frontera de México fue más difficil, crossing into México was the most dificult, we crossed through the mountains y nos asaltaron, ne robaron todo, they attacked us, they robbed us of everything, they attacked us. ¡Los banditos, los narcos!

PEDRA: ¡En Guatemala, yo llore tres noches! Miraba todo, la luz, la luna. Estaba llorando al Señor.

CANDELA: I also cried for three nights, for many nights, the last night I was watching everything, for the last time, the light, the moon, I was crying ....

ANITA: The last time, the last night!

CHORUS (*Making large gestures of grief, desperation, in a stylized, operatic way, moving rhythmically and chanting*): Qué paso, qué paso, ¿qué paso la última noche? ¿La última vez? What happened, what happened the last night, the last time?

> *Characters act out the different scenarios of the last moments before everybody's departures in flashback, dream like sequences. With each, we are transported to their respective homes and countries. The characters are both acting out their own departures and presenting the scene to the audience, like an offering. The retelling and reliving is a joint effort as all characters identify with each other's stories, even though they differ from one another.*

CHORUS¡: Las despedidas! Odio las despedidas. The farewells, the adios, the goodbyes. I hate farewells!

Dreamscape or flashback scene back in México, the night before Ysabel is planning to leave her family and her two small children.

YSABEL (*Toward the audience. For the first time she is focused on her own story instead of the others*): Yo decidí irme porque podíamos dar una mejor vida a mis hijos. I decided to leave so I can give a better life to my children, it was May. Recuerdo esa noche, era la última noche ... I remember that night, it was the last night ... Only thinking that it was the last night ... me da mucho dolor en mi corazón, it gives me so much pain in my heart. I had to say goodbye to my children, my son was four and my daughter was six. I remember I lay next to my son in bed ... I was caressing him, lo acariciaba, I barely slept that night ... and he said ...

> *She is lying down, reliving the moment next to her son.*

¿Mama, porque no te vas en tu cama? ¿mama why don't you go to your bed?' And I said to myself: no sabes hijo, you don't know son, that I won't be here in the morning ... Mi hija, my daughter tenia calentura, she had a fever, she knew that she won't see me in the morning. ¡Fue tan difícil!

> *Gets up and relives saying goodbye to the rest of her family, her sister, parents and grandparents.*

Adiós, adiós, hermana, mama y papa, abuelo y abuela, adiós a todos, voy a regresar ... I will return ...

> *Toward the audience.*

¡Fue tan duro, tan duro! Yo no quise despedir-me, I didn't want to say good-bye to my sister and my parents and my grandparents, because I thought I would return.

> *The other characters become her family, waving goodbye in slow waves. The moment has to last a while to render the intensity of the wrenching goodbyes and to become almost unbearable for the audience.*

CHORUS: Adiós Ysabel, adiós querida, cuida-te, take care of yourself, adiós, adiós, adiós, adiós.

YSABEL: Recuerdo que yo sali de casa llorando, I left the house crying, people were watching us, but I didn't care, what I was living was so hard ...

> *All the following separation scenes have to be acted at a fast pace, with urgency and desperation.*

MERCEDES (*Speaking directly to the audience*): Yo me despedí de mi hijo que tenía 14 años, y él dijo antes de irme, dijo ... When I said good-bye to my son, he was 14, he said, he said *(Reliving the scene, one of the actors is playing the son)*: ¿Mama porque te vas? ¡No te vayas por favor! Mama, why are you leaving? Don't go please!' I said: 'me voy porque tu vida sea mejor, I'm going so that your life can be better ...'

CHORUS: No te vayas mama, porque te vas, why are you leaving, don't go!

> *Waving good-bye in synchronized movements.*

She is going, she is leaving, adiós, Mercedes, adiós, adiós, adiós.

MERCEDES (*Speaking to the audience, filled with grief*): Él se murió a los 15 años en un accidente ... no lo pude ver. I never saw him again. ¡Que dolor!

CHORUS (*In shock, but also in sympathy with Mercedes's grief*): Oohhh no! Tu hijo se murió, se murió, he died and you never saw him again, ¡que dolor!

ANITA: Lo más difícil fue ... tener que abandonar su tierra, todo está aquí, toda mi vida está aquí. The hardest of all was to leave my earth, everything was there, all my life was there.

CHORUS: Si, dejar su tierra y su familia. Despedirse de todo, todo, todo. Yes, leaving one's earth and family. To say farewell to everything, everything, everything ... adios, adiós, adiós.

As in the previous reenactments, all the characters are waving good-bye to Anita. Images of large groups of people with bags, backpacks and suitcases leaving Honduras, Guatemala, México can be projected.

¡Adiós ANITA! Adiós, adiós, no nos olvides, ¡don't forget us!

MATEO: ¡Adiós abuelo, adiós, mis hijos, mi esposa, mis hermanos! ¡Yo me voy, adiós! (*Towards the audience*): That was the hardest thing, to say goodbye to my children, my wife, my brothers!

CHORUS: ¡Adiós Mateo, adiós! ¡No nos olvides, cuida-te! Don't forget us, take care of yourself!

PEDRA: ¡Adiós, hermanas, adiós abuela!

CHORUS: ¡Adiós Pedra, vaya con Dios!

CANDELA: ¡Adiós abuela, adiós, hermanos!

YSABEL: ¡Adiós, hijos, adiós mama, papa, hermana!

ANITA: ¡Adiós a todo y a todos!

CHORUS: Adiós, adiós, adiós, cuida-te, take care of yourself, take your suitcase, ¡la maleta!

A growing frenzy takes over everybody on stage, characters are saying goodbyes and adios, running, waving, crying. The scene must become hallucinatory, moving at a dizzying pace. After a while it all stops and everybody stands frozen in the moment of departure, holding a suitcase, a bag, or carrying a backpack. The song La despedida by Ana Gabriel is played.

End of TABLEAU II

(*Blackout. Music continues through blackout*)

TABLEAU III

How Did You Cross the Border?

?Cómo cruzaste la Frontera?

The characters present their encounters with the Coyotes to the audience and the scene is acted as a dreamscape. The atmosphere is dark, menacing, sinister. The actor playing Coyote plays all the coyotes in everybody's crossing.

CHORUS: It was like this. Así fue, this is the story, esta es la historia, toda nuestra historia. Recuerdo muy bien, I remember well, recuerdo ... no se puede olvidar, you can't forget it ...

CANDELA: ¡A la frontera de Sonora the Coyote picked us up! It was like this, así fue!

COYOTE (*Whispers in her ear conspiratorially*): ¡Recuerda la clave! Remember the password! You will meet someone who takes you across. ¡El dinero!

CANDELA (*Candela hands him a package with money in silence*):

...

COYOTE: Keep going, someone will meet you on the way, give them the password. ¿Nada más, entiendes?

CANDELA: Tenía mucho miedo, I was so scared, but I kept going. Others joined me on the way through the desert. Hacía mucho frío it was so cold, I felt sick, I didn't know then that I was pregnant.

ANITA: After we were attacked on the road we went to a house, casa hogar, a safety house only it wasn't safe, no era nada seguro.

COYOTE: You'll stay here till morning. Someone will take you across the river. ¡El dinero!

ANITA (*Anita hands him a package with money in silence*): I was afraid in the casa hogar, there were bad people. I felt bad for my brother, to see all the guns y machetes. Earlier I crossed río Bravo. I can't swim, la necesidad y el temor fue más fuerte, fear was stronger, my brother and I cruzamos the river looking for the shallow parts, we thought it was over, but then the hardest part came, with the Coyote. Need pushes you to do things you never thought you would ... like crossing a river without knowing how to swim!

MERCEDES: Era demasiado cansada, I was too tired, no quería caminar más después dos meses de caminar y vivir en los potreros. I didn't want to walk any more after all the walking and living in the mountains for two months. I thought of my son who said: "mama no te vayas, porque te vas?" I pray and cry and pray and walk, then Coyote take us to casa hogar ... for a lot of money, todo el dinero que yo tenía, all the money I had ...

> *Mercedes hands Coyote a stack of notes for the next crossing.*

PEDRA (*Pedra hands Coyote a package with money*): ¡Nade por el río par atrás! After I swam down the river we walked some more, there were other people. Coyote helped us at first, took us across the border with México, then we met another Coyote to help us cross la frontera de los Estados Unidos, then ... pues ...

COYOTE (*Coyote gives her a larger package*): Take this, put it inside your backpack! You give it to the person in the house, entiendes?

PEDRA: ¿Qué es? ¡No quiero meterme en problemas!
(*Towards the audience*): I didn't want any trouble, I didn't want
to carry the package, I had a bad feeling!

COYOTE (*Laughs cynically*): You are already in trouble, you
are crossing the border illegally. This is the least de tus
problemas. You don't take it, you don't cross.

PEDRA: Necessity makes you do things you never thought you
would do. Nunca en la vida. Tenía tanto miedo.

YSABEL: Es cierto, it's true. Cómo yo, cómo yo y mi marido,
like me and my husband when we left our house y nuestra
familia in Oaxaca. We took the plane to Tijuana and went to
una zona de Tijuana muy fea, muy peligrosa, we went to an area
in Tijuana that was ugly, dangerous. Llegamos a un hotel to go
to the ciudad de Tecate. They were going to call us at three in
the morning.

CHORUS: Ay, mi hija, at three in the morning, muy temprano,
so early, it must have been scary.

YSABEL: Crossing the city of Tijuana, I was sorprendida to see
so many ugly things.

CHORUS: ¿Cómo que Ysabel, like what, like what?

YSABEL: Cómo gente drogada, prostitutas, people on drugs,
prostitues, other things de que no quiero hablar, I don't want to
talk about it ... We went to a house with three other men, all in
the same room, I was so scared, I couldn't sleep, no pude
dormir. I was the only woman. ¡La misma necesidad nos empuja
hacer cosas que nunca habían pensado hacer!

CHORUS: Es verdad, necessity pushes you to do things that you never thought you would do.

YSABEL: We went to the mountains in Tecate to cross. We started to climb, era muy frío, it was so cold ... I had doubts, I wanted to return, quería regresar ... La ciudad de Tecate con las montañas alrededor ... todo me sembraba muy raro, the city of Tecate, the mountains, everything seemd strange. I was shivering from the cold at three in the morning, mirando el amanecer watching the sunrise ... surrounded by people I didn't know, with men I didn't know ...

COYOTE: Andale, andale, que se mueve, go, ¡go, move! Me han robado los pollos. El otro cabrón me robo la gente ... The other asshole stole my people ... Now you pay more. We go to casa de los pollos, ahora! Now I said! Move!

YSABEL: ¿Dónde vamos? Where are we going?

COYOTE: I told you, to the safety house. We have to get more people; I'm meeting someone at the casa. We need to get the people, no entiendes? Andale!

> *He urges Ysabel and the other people to move on to the "casa de los pollos," so called safety house. Coyote puts a gun to the head of one of the fugitives and makes him take a package.*

You carry this across cabrón or we kill your family back in México, hear me?

> *The person takes the package in silence and puts it at the bottom of his backpack. Then Coyote does the same with two other members of the group. They all take the packages and hide them in their backpacks.*

MERCEDES: There are many coyotes and not all tienen las mismas intenciones, not all have the same intentions, to just help people cross the border.

PEDRA: Sometimes they deal drugs and they ask the people to carry the drugs for them, ser la mula. They threaten they will kill their family if they refuse to be the mule. They work for the narcotraficantes!

MATEO: ¡En la frontera, at this border ... drugs, prostitution, tráfico de personas, el abuso, physical and mental abuse, all the bad things, todo malo, todo malo!

CHORUS: Sí, todo malo aquí a la frontera, all bad things at the border. We just want to cross the border, sin nada malo, without anything bad, it's why we are leaving, por eso nos vamos de nuestro país, por eso!

> *The group walks across the stage, more strenuously, climbing a difficult mountain path.*

YSABEL: Caminamos y caminamos y caminamos, we walk, and we walk, and we walk, the road is hard up the mountain.

CANDELA: It's six in the morning, Coyote needs more people. He meets another coyote, un joven de 20 años. Me siento muy mal, I feel sick, I'm thirsty and hungry all the time, todo me duele, everything hurts.

ANITA: ¡Hace mucho frío! Coyote is looking for more people. Sometimes there are wars between the Coyotes, and they steal each other's people, they call the ones they cross al otro lado "pollos." It's so cold, we run, and we hide.

COYOTE: ¿Dónde está la gente? ¿Dónde están todos? ¡Salga todos! Where is everybody, out, out all of you!

YSABEL: ¡Y la gente empezaron a salir de los árboles, la naturaleza, niños de 14 años, then people start coming out from behind the trees, the plants, 14-year-old children trembling de frío, wearing casi nada, wearing almost nothing! ¡Hace mucho frío, it's so cold and all the people are coming out from behind the vegetation, muy raro, so strange!

COYOTE: ¡Bueno, this is better, mucho mejor, twenty five people, mucho mejor! ¡Ahora cruzamos al otro lado, now we cross to the other side! ¡Muévase, andale!

> *The group walks again, with Ysabel in the front.*
> *Then they stop abruptly at a sign of Coyote.*

¡Estamos en los Estados Unidos! We are in the US. Now comes the hardest part. The border patrols are everywhere. When I say run, you run, fast as you can. When I say bajo tierra, you go down on the ground. ¡Corre, corre, corre! Un mosco, a helicopter, hide, a bajo los arbustos y plantas, down, next to the plants, down, down, down.

> *All throw themselves to the ground.*

Get up, go, now it's our chance to go, ahora, corre!

> *All run again.*

Stop, I said stop!

> *All stop.*

¡Vamos a cruzar la carretera, we'll cross the highway, you'll be the first one, corre lo más rapido que tú puedes, run as fast as you can! When I say down you go down, when I say run, you run. We have to get to the highway, run!

YSABEL: Nunca hice esto en mi vida, I never did this in my life. These coyotes never get tired, they can walk or drive for 20 hours without stopping. He said run, we run, he said get down, we go down.

MATEO: The coyotes would do anything for money, anything, lo que sea!

YSABEL: I am the first one in the group. We run, my husband encuentra una cobija, he finds a blanket and uses this blanket to erase our footprints in the desert so the border patrol can't follow us.

MERCEDES: ¡Dios mio que oscuridad! When the light of the border patrol moves over us, we go down, then we run again.

PEDRA: It's so dark, we can't see a thing, we run in the dark, a woman falls down, I help her get up, she is shaking, no veo nada, I can't see a thing.

COYOTE: Now is the time to cross la carretera! Go, stop when I say stop. ¡Ahora! A car will be coming on the highway, a truck. ¡Run, stop when you see the car, get in the car lo más rapido que puedes, as fast as you can!

> *All run as fast as they can with Ysabel in the front. The sound of a car screeching to a halt. All are getting inside the car quickly, piled up on top of each other, two people get inside the trunk.*

We have to get out and run again, there is a raid. Stop, get out and run in that direction!

The sound of car screeching to a halt again. All get out of the car and run again.

YSABEL: It's so dark, no puedo ver nada, I can't see where I'm going.

CHORUS: We can't see a thing, it's so dark, it's so cold, seguimos corriendo y corriendo, we keep running and running in the dark!

COYOTE: Don't talk, run ahead. We'll get to a little river, tenemos que cruzar-lo, we have to cross it. Take off your pants and shoes and carry them above your head. ¡Corre!

All run in great confusion in the dark, bumping into each other, they get to the river, some take off their shoes and pants, Ysabel keeps her shoes on but she takes off a pair of pants and has another one underneath that she keeps on. They cross the river.

YSABEL: I lost one of my shoes. I have to find my shoe, I put my money in it.

Toward the Chorus Member playing her husband.

Corre tu, you run! (*Towards the audience*): I tell my husband to run and leave me behind, I can't run anymore ...

CHORUS MEMBER (*Playing Ysabel's husband*): No, yo no te dejo aquí, I won't leave you here, let's look for your shoe. ¡Yo no te dejo!

YSABEL: ¿Ay, yo sentí un animal, I heard an animal, what can it be?

CHORUS MEMBER (*Acting as Ysabel's husband*): No es nada, it's nothing, aquí esta tu zapto, Here is your shoe!

YSABEL: ¡Gracias a dios that I find it, here is the dinero, I find it!

> *Gestures towards Coyote and hands him the money in her shoe.*

COYOTE: ¡It's wet, que carajo! What the fuck, I told you to keep your valuables and shoes above the water, didn't I? Give it here!

> *Takes the money from Ysabel, blows on it and puts it in his coat pocket.*

See the house over there at the other side of the highway? That's where we have to get, run, corre, corre, fast as you can!

YSABEL (*Towards the audience, more breathlessly than before*): We get to the other safety house, a mobile home! Coyote calls someone on his phone and speaks in code, no entiendo nada, I don't understand a thing.

ANITA: He smells of marijuana. A single mother with two children live in the house, she does this for money, she keeps refugees who just crossed the border.

YSABEL: We all sleep on the floor, I sleep next to the woman's younger child, en el piso, he also sleeps on the floor. She feeds us once a day.

CANDELA: We stay here for five days. Tengo tanta hambre, I am so hungry. The men eat nothing, only smoke, only the women and the children eat.

YSABEL: Sometimes I regret my decision to leave. Estreno a mis hijos, pero I don't cry even if I miss my children so much.

PEDRA: Un niño llore en la noche, una mujer llore en la noche, a child is crying at night, a woman is crying at night.

CHORUS: Lagrimas, muchas lágrimas esta noche fría ... many, many tears, this cold, cold night.

MERCEDES (*To the audience*): Cinco días en la casa hogar, fue una pesadilla. A nightmare ... in the safety house for five days, sleeping on the floor, eating once a day. Yo llore al señor toda la noche, I cried all night. I cried and prayed. Bad things happened in the house, people came and went. Llore al Señor para las otras mujeres y para mis hijos, I cry and pray all night for the other women and for my children.

PEDRA (*Whispering to Ysabel in the night. All whisper while lying on the floor*): ¿Qué hacemos aquí, sabes? Do you know why we are here?

YSABEL: No sé, I think we are waiting for the other guide, or maybe for COYOTE to get us las cartas, the id cards ...

ANITA: If I knew all this, no me hubiera ido ... I wouldn't have left ...

MERCEDES: ¡Ni yo tampoco! Me neither! ¡Ay, hijas, que pesadilla, what a nightmare! I should have listened to my son, me dije no te vayas por favor mama, he told me don't go mama, Please don't go!

CANDELA: What if we run away and cross on our own? I can't stay here any longer. Me siento muy mal. I feel sick.

YSABEL: Escuchen todos, listen no hay nada que hacer, there is nothing else to do, we won't make it on our own, we paid him, he has to do what he promised, esperamos un poquito más, todo va a estar bien ... it's going to be alright, let's just wait till tomorrow.

ANITA: ¡Si esperemos hasta la mañana!

CANDELA: Hace mucho frío. So cold! ¡Voy a morir hasta la mañana! I'm going to die till morning.

MATEO: ¡Tome mi cobija, here ... take my blanket!

CHORUS MEMBER *(Playing Ysabel's husband towards Ysabel)*: Y tu también, take my blanket, todo bien.

YSABEL: Give it to the niño.

MERCEDES: ¡Si, dar mi cobija a los niños! Give my blanket to the children. Estoy bien.

ANITA: Mujeres, if we lie close to each other we warm up.

PEDRA: Tiene razón, there is room para dos personas más in this corner.

YSABEL: Y aquí también, hay espacio, next to the niño, he is shivering too, let's stay close to each other, there is more room next to the child.

> *Talks to the audience again.*

The cold is the worst of all, el peor de todo, peor que el hambre, worse than hunger. Another woman comes to get the money, es la novia del Coyote, Coyote's girlfriend, es muy fria, she is a cold woman, only cares about money. She and Coyote eat in front of us, we don't eat, she only wants our dinero.

CHORUS (The following lines are staggered, the last line is said by all at once):

Tenemos hambre,

tenemos frio,

tenemos miedo

We are hungry,

we are cold,

we are afraid,

Esperamos la madrugada,

we are waiting for morning,

el amanecer vendrá pronto,

the sun will rise soon, esperamos, esperamos ...

COYOTE (*Goes to each one and collects more money*): Tomorrow you get your fake green cards! ¡Bienvenidos a los Estados Unidos! Welcome to the United States!

(Coyote leaves the stage. All others lie down, they stay still, only their breathing is heard. Sounds of coyotes howling in the night)

End of TABLEAU III

(Blackout. The song El Desierto sung by Lhasa de Sela is Heard in blackout)

TABLEAU IV

Bienvenidos a los Estados Unidos

Welcome to the United States

A wire fence separates the asylum seekers from the audience. It looks like a cage. Immigration Officer is standing in front of them.

IMMIGRATION OFFICER: If you don't have papers you'll be deported, you know that, right? If you have fake papers, you'll be deported, you know that, right? You should be deported anyways if you ask me! Go back to your countries, go back to where you came from, go back to your shithole countries. Stand up, all of you, stand up, come over here. I said stand up, come over here! Are you deaf or something?

> *Immigrants stand up slowly like in a dream and do what he says, lining up along the fence, and facing the audience.*

IMMIGRATION OFFICER: Name, nationality and papers. Each one of you, name, nationality, date of arrival and papers. Go ...

YSABEL: My name is YSA ...

IMMIGRATION OFFICER (*Interrupting her*): Did I ask you? Keep quiet!

YSABEL: I thought ...

IMMIGRATION OFFICER: Shut up, you don't think, you do what I say! You. Name, nationality, date of arrival, papers!

Addressing Mercedes

MERCEDES: MERCEDES FERNANDEZ. ¡De HONDURAS! Llego el 13 de septiembre, 2010. ¡No tengo papeles!

IMMIGRATION OFFICER: English! Any of you here bright people speak English?

Ysabel raises her hand that she does speak English.

IMMIGRATION OFFICER: What did she say?

YSABEL: Her name is Mercedes Fernandez. She ...

IMMIGRATION OFFICER: I got that much, you idiot! What else?

YSABEL: She is from Honduras, she arrived 13th September 2017. She has no papers!

IMMIGRATION OFFICER (*Imitating and mocking her*): She is from Honduras; she has no papers ... I no speak English, ... I criminal from shithole country ... I come to America to steal and rape ... I make many children in America to get more benefits, I take jobs from American people, blah, blah, blah ...

Changes tone to angry and violent, yelling at the group.

What did I say, hm, what did I just ask you assholes? One by one, in order: name, nationality, date of arrival, papers! No papers, deported, fake papers, deported ... Honduras mama, here, no papers, no asylum. Comprende?

The refugees say their names and nationalities one after the other, breathlessly, mechanically.

MATEO: MATEO Dominguez, from México, el 26 de agosto 2017, ¡sin papeles!

PEDRA: PEDRA Fernandez, Honduras, el 15 de octubre,2017, ¡no tengo documentos!

CANDELA: CANDELA Rodriguez, México, el 10 de mayo 2017, ¡no tengo papeles!

ANITA: ANITA Dominguez, de Guatemala, el 15 de mayo, 2018, ¡sin documentos!

YSABEL: YSABEL Delgado, from México, el 7 de junio, 2017, ¡I have green card!

IMMIGRATION OFFICER: Let me see, translator of the year, ha, ha, it's fake! You'll be deported, smart ass, as will all of you bunch of delinquents with your coyotes and drug dealings!

All refugees huddle and whisper a plan to each other.

YSABEL: Eso no es cierto. Tenemos derechos, vamos a pedir un abogado. My brother who is in Los Estados Unidos told me that if they threaten with deportation, we have to be silent and ask for a lawyer!

> *Turns to the audience and translates for them in whispers.*

That's not true. We have rights, we'll ask for a lawyer, my brother told me that if they threaten with deportation, we have to be silent and ask for a lawyer!

IMMIGRATION OFFICER: Stop whispering, shut up, or are you in a hurry to be sent back to your shithole countries?

> *They become the Chorus again and stand together in a consolidated group in front of the fence, facing the audience. They stand in silence. Images of camps at the border and immigrants behind fences should be projected. The scene has to be dark and disturbing.*

CHORUS: Tenemos derechos, we have rights, pedimos un abogado, we are asking for a lawyer, tenemos derechos, we have rights!

IMMIGRATION OFFICER (*Throws a bucket of cold water at them.*)

CHORUS (*In a chant, rhythmically*): Derechos, abogado, derechos, abogado, we have rights, we want a lawyer, we have rights, ¡we want a lawyer!

IMMIGRATION OFFICER (*Throws another bucket of water at them, then pokes each one of them with the gun. Chorus remains standing, unphased*): Here, I give you your stupid lawyer, see this, here are your rights, here, take these rights, how do you like it?

> *Everybody freezes. A voice over is heard with news sound bites while images of politicians visiting border camps are being projected. The soundbites become more and more accelerated, some overlap, until all is heard is a general din and mixture of disparate words and sentences from news channels.*

VOICE: ... humanitarian crisis ... Twenty-five hundred children were separated from their families ... The president defended his executive order ... the court caseload on the increasing number of migrants, mostly from Central America, who are seeking asylum ... the attorney general defended the president's executive order ... the unprecedented influx of migrants from México and Central America ... the vice president visited detention centers at the border ... defended the actions of the president ... defended the actions of the president ... defended the actions of the president ... Democratic presidential candidate visited the detention centers ... condemned the conditions ... condemned the unsanitary conditions ... the justice department defended the conditions ... the president tweeted ... the president sent another incendiary tweet ... the children don't need toothbrushes and soap ... one month old infant unwashed for ten days ... the president defended ... three children died in US custody ... inhumane conditions... human rights violations ... Democratic candidate compared detention centers to

concentration camps ... drew criticism from members of
GOP ... Congress requested hearings ... White House defended
its actions ... Press Secretary defended the president's
measures ... Press Secretary was asked by owner of restaurant in
small Virginia town to leave the premises ... restaurant owner
received death threats ... Press Secretary was discriminated
against ... asked to leave ... restaurant owner stood by her
decision ... small town in Virginia ... the President condemned,
the President condemned... threatened ... tweeted ...
threatened ...

> *Blackout. Muffled voices, cries, orders are heard in
> the dark. The blackout lasts for several seconds to
> create unease and even terror. When lights are up, the
> stage is empty, the wire fence has disappeared. Ysabel
> comes first on the stage and makes signs to the others
> who are backstage to come over. The atmosphere has
> changed to a brighter and more relaxed one.*

YSABEL: ¡Venga, venga, es seguro, no tengas miedo! Come,
don't be scared, it's safe. Bring all the food. ¡Aquí está bien, in
back of the house!

> *When a character starts speaking before the other has
> finished, the point of interruption is marked /.*

CANDELA: ¡Extraño la comida de mi país! /I miss the food
from my country!

PEDRA: ¡I miss my abuela!

MATEO: Extraño a mis hijos, /a mi esposa, a mi abuelo ...

MERCEDES: Extraño todo, todo de mi país ... /I miss
everything ...

ANITA: ¡Extraño a mis padres y a mi tierra natal!

YSABEL: I miss my children, my sister, my parents, todos y todo! Pero siento que van a poder venir aquí pronto, maybe they come here soon ...

CANDELA: It's been a year already. I had my baby, gracias a Dios. /No puedo creer that I crossed when I was pregnant...

MATEO: It feels like a long time ... So much happened, bueno y malo, ¡los dos!

MERCEDES: Extraño mucho a mi hijo que se murió en el accidente. ¡Que dolor! Se murió en un accidente ... no lo pude ver. I miss my son who died in the accident after I leave, I miss him so much. I never saw him again ... When I come here, I am crying so much, I didn't want to eat or do anything. Y un día el Señor me lo envió en un sueño, it gave me peace to see him in the dream, he was in the light and smiling.

CHORUS: ¡Che dolor perder su hijo! He was smiling in your dream! ¡Que dolor!

PEDRA: Señora Mercedes siempre ayuda a las otras madres que han perdido hijos.

ANITA: ¡Así es! ¡Mercedes always helps the mothers who lost children and also the mujeres abusadas! She helps all abused women from church.

MATEO: Señora Mercedes, estamos siempre aquí con usted. /And you have your other children aquí.

PEDRA: Así es, we are here with you Señora Mercedes.

CANDELA: Mi hijo is already one year old. Entiende un poquito inglés y Español, he understands Spanish and English.

YSABEL: El tiempo se va muy rápido, ¿verdad? Vamos, eat, eat, los nopales son muy sabrosos, the cactus is very good y los frijoles también. No es malo, it's not too bad living in Virginia.

MATEO: Al menos tenemos trabajos.

YSABEL: Es cierto, at least we have work, ¡and it's safer here than in the big city ... cómo por ejemplo New York!

PEDRA: Mateo, yo siempre quise preguntarte, I always want to ask, what did you do with the paquetes from Coyote that time in the safety house?

MATEO: Cuando Coyote came al amanecer con las cartas de social security, another man was supposed to come for the mercancía and he never come. Maybe they kill him, no sé. I dropped the paquetes in the valley. Pero, I don't like to talk about this.

MERCEDES: ¡El Señor vigilaba sobre de ti! God was watching you. I pray for you that night in the casa hogar.

PEDRA: ¡Eso es cierto! Señora Mercedes always pray for everybody and God always listen to her.

YSABEL: Pero todo eso es en el pasado, it's all in the past. We are safe here. /No hay Coyote, no hay narcotraficantes!

CANDELA: ¡Pero hay ICE! ¡Son peor que los narcotraficantes! ¡Esperamos que no venga ICE! Let's hope ICE isn't coming over here ...

MERCEDES: ¡Ojalá ... I hope so too! ¡Pero yo no tengo miedo! /After all that happen to me, I am not scared of anything.

PEDRA: ¡Nada es perfecto, pero it's safer here than in Honduras!

ANITA: ¡Y más seguro que Guatemala! ¡Pero no es fácil ser inmigrante!

YSABEL: It's true, it's not easy being an immigrant. Era muy difícil at first for me and my husband, nadie hablaba Español aquí, not like New York where many people speak Spanish, everybody stared at us. When we moved to the house from the church, we didn't have furniture. We searched in the trash for a bed, that was our first bed, nuestra primera cama, no puedo olvidar eso.

ANITA: ¡Ay Ysabel, yo no sabía eso, you never talk about it, pobrecita! Yo también, I was muy sola in the beginning. Sometimes people stare at me! ¡Me siento raro, I feel strange!

CANDELA: Me too, when I enter a restaurant con mi hijo! One time they make me feel very bad ... I had to leave. It's better now, that I know more English ... Pero I'm afraid of ICE, I hear some people from church are sent back.

MERCEDES: ¡La gente con las banderas confederadas es muy rara! / No entiendo, que quiere esa gente?

ANITA: Si es cierto, you are right Señora Mercedes. I don't get the people with the weird flags either, what do they want? They have guns too. / Tengo miedo for my brother in school.

PEDRA: Yes, they have guns and then they smile. Everybody smiles here ... too much! No todos que sonrían son amables. Not all who smile are kind!

MATEO: ¡Esta bien! Me, I like smiling! It makes me happy to smile to people.

YSABEL: It's better now! Having to smile is not so bad! / Some people both smile and are kind!

MATEO: ¡A mí me gusta aquí! I like it here.

YSABEL: ¡Mateo siempre sees el lado positivo always! We have to make it matter, ... estar juntos, help each other ... help the newcomers.

PEDRA: Pero sin ti, without you Ysabel we couldn't have done it ... it's all thanks to you ...

MERCEDES: Eso es cierto Ysabel, it's true, you always help us, que Dios te bendiga.

MATEO: Tu organización es estupenda Ysabel.

ANITA: Yes, your organization es increíble. Always helping the new people ...

CANDELA: Protecting the new ones from the raids ... letting us know ...

MERCEDES: Translating for us at the hospital ...

MATEO: Driving us muy temprano at five in the morning when we have interview with inmigración ...

CANDELA: When I had my baby, you took me to the hospital and stay with me until the baby was born!

PEDRA: ¡Tu sufriste mucho y ayudas a todo el mundo! You help everybody!

YSABEL: We all suffered, señora Mercedes lost her son, eso es el peor de todo, worse than all of us, Mateo left his wife and children, Pedra left her parents and abuela, Anita her sisters, we all suffered, and it is a little better every day ...

ANITA: ¡Pero todavía no tenemos papeles!

PEDRAL: Es verdad, we still don't have real papers.

CANDELA: I don't know what will happen with us ... ¡Tengo miedo para mi niño!

ANITA: No te preocupes Candela, we support each other, we have lawyers, gracias a Ysabel, todo va a estar bien.

YSABEL: Si, todo bien. Aquí estamos en Virginia, all together. Esta tan oscuro aquí de noche, it's much darker at night here than in the big city. ¿Recuerdo when we crosed the border, crosed the river, walked in the desert, ... this is how dark it was ... recuerdan?

MATEO: I remember, pero no veo nada, I don't see a thing ...

YSABEL: ¡Mira la luna! The moon is coming out. ¡La misma luna!

MERCEDES: ¡La luna y las estrellas cómo mi última noche en Honduras! Here you can see, the moon, the stars ...

ANITA: ¡Cómo mi última noche en Guatemala! My last night in Guatemala!

YSABEL: My last night in México, I never forget, ¡nunca olvidare!

CHORUS: ¡Cómo la última noche en nuestro país! Aquí en Virginia podemos ver la luna y las estrellas. Here we can see the moon and the stars. The same stars, the same earth. ¡Las mismas estrellas, la misma tierra!

PEDRA: Escucha, una sirena ...

ANITA: La luz, get down, the light.

MERCEDES: Es una redada ... ¡No tengas miedo!

CHORUS: ¿A raid, Dios mio, another raid, it never ends, cuando terminara, ¿cuándo terminara?

CANDELA: Mi hijo, I have to take my son to the neighbor, she promise to take care of him if they send me back ...

YSABEL: Tranquila ... todo va a estar bien .... ¡Corre!

MATEO: ¡Don't be afraid! We lived worse things!

YSABEL: Run inside my house! ¡Rápido! Run as fast as you can! Run!

CHORUS: Corre, corre,

¡Lo más rápido que puedes! ¡Corre!

Corre, corremos, ¡más rápido!

Las montañas, los ríos, las carreteras

¡Siempre corremos!

> *Blackout. The song Paloma Negra sung by Chavela Vargas plays in the dark.*

END OF PLAY

Author Bios

Christine Evans (Introduction): Christine Evans' plays have been produced in her native Australia, the US, Canada, the UK, Austria and New Zealand. Productions and reading venues include the Royal Shakespeare Company, Arts Above (London), Playbox Theater (UK), Chocolate Moose Theater (Montreal), the Sydney Opera House, Belvoir Street Theater (Australia) and many others. Her play *Trojan Barbie* premiered at the American Repertory Theater and has over thirty subsequent productions. *Trojan Barbie* won the Jane Chambers Award, the "Plays for the 21ˢ Century" Award, was a Griffin Award finalist and is published by Samuel French (UK and US). Her novel-in-verse, *Cloudless,* was released by UWA Publishing (2015). www.christineevanswriter.com

Julia Pascal (Foreword): Dr Julia Pascal is a London-based playwright, theatre director and scholar. She is a Visiting Research Fellow in the Department of English within the Faculty of Arts and Humanities at King's College London and Associate Research Fellow in the school of Arts (Birkbeck Centre for Contemporary Theatre). Her dramas explore exiles and those living on the margins of society. Pascal's grandparents were of Jewish Romanian and Lithuanian backgrounds and their histories have inspired much of her stage work. She has written 18 plays most of which are published and have been produced nationally and internationally. These include *The Holocaust Trilogy, Nineveh, The Yiddish Queen Lear, Crossing Jerusalem* and *Woman In The Moon.* Currently Julia is writing *As Happy As God In France* where the leading characters are Hannah Arendt and Charlotte Salomon. Julia's stage career includes working as an actor in theatre, radio, television and film Her awards have included a NESTA Dreamtime Fellowship, an Alfred Bradley BBC Award, Moondance Award and she was a finalist in the Association for Theatre in Higher Education

Award of Excellence in Playwriting. In 2017, Julia was nominated for the Gilder/Coigney International Theatre Award as a member of the League of International Theatre Women. As director of Pascal Theatre Company, Julia also produces large scale projects that are artistic and educational."

Domnica Radulescu (Playwright): is an American writer of Romanian origin, living in the United States where she arrived in 1983 as a political refugee. She lives, functions, and writes in the hyphenated spaces between cultures, languages, and artistic universes. Radulescu is the author of three critically acclaimed and best-selling novels, *Train to Trieste* (Knopf 2008 &2009), *Black Sea Twilight* (Transworld 2011 & 2012) and *Country of Red Azaleas* (Hachette 2016) and of award-winning plays. Her play *Exile Is My Home* was produced off, off Broadway, at the Theater for the New City in New York, in 2016, and its production was nominated for an Innovative Theater Award, and received the Outstanding Performance by an Ensemble Cast Award from the Hispanic Organization of Latin Actors. Radulescu's first novel *Train to Trieste* was translated into thirteen languages and received the Best Fiction Award from the Library of Virginia in 2009. She is twice a Fulbright scholar and winner of the 2011 Outstanding Faculty Award from the State of Virginia. She is working on her fourth novel, a political thriller about the Romanian Holocaust, titled *My Father's Orchards*. She is also working on a collaborative theater project about women survivors of sexual and racially motived violence titled *Moon Drops. Channeling and Healing Trauma through Theater.* Radulescu published twelve non-fiction books, edited and co-edited collections on topics ranging from the tragic heroine in western literature to feminist comedy, to studies of exile literature to theater of war and exile. Radulescu is Distinguished Service Professor of Comparative Literature in

Lexington, Virginia. She holds a PhD in French and Italian literature from the University of Chicago.

http://www.domnicaradulescu.com/

https://en.wikipedia.org/wiki/Domnica_Radulescu

Made in the USA
Columbia, SC
23 January 2021